quilting with
FAT
QUARTERS

17 new patterns from
the staff at That Patchwork Place®

Martingale®
Create with Confidence

Quilting with Fat Quarters: 17 New Patterns from the
Staff at That Patchwork Place®
© 2012 by Martingale®

Martingale
19021 120th Ave. NE, Ste. 102
Bothell, WA 98011-9511 USA
www.martingale-pub.com

Mission Statement

Dedicated to providing quality products
and service to inspire creativity.

Credits

President & CEO: Tom Wierzbicki

Editor in Chief: Mary V. Green

Design Director: Paula Schlosser

Managing Editor: Karen Costello Soltys

Technical Editor: Christine Barnes

Copy Editor: Sheila Chapman Ryan

Production Manager: Regina Girard

Illustrator: Laurel Strand

Cover & Text Designer: Shelly Garrison

Photographer: Brent Kane

Printed in China

17 16 15 14 13 12   8 7 6 5 4 3 2 1

**Library of Congress Cataloging-in-Publication
Data is available upon request.**

ISBN: 978-1-60468-186-4

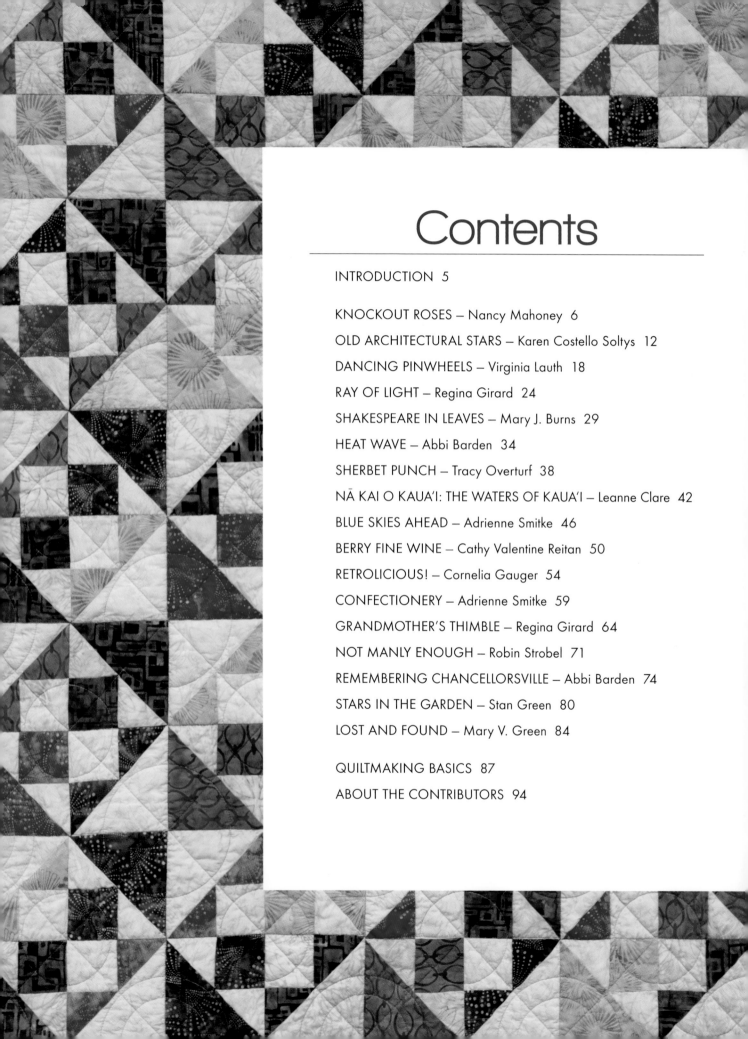

Contents

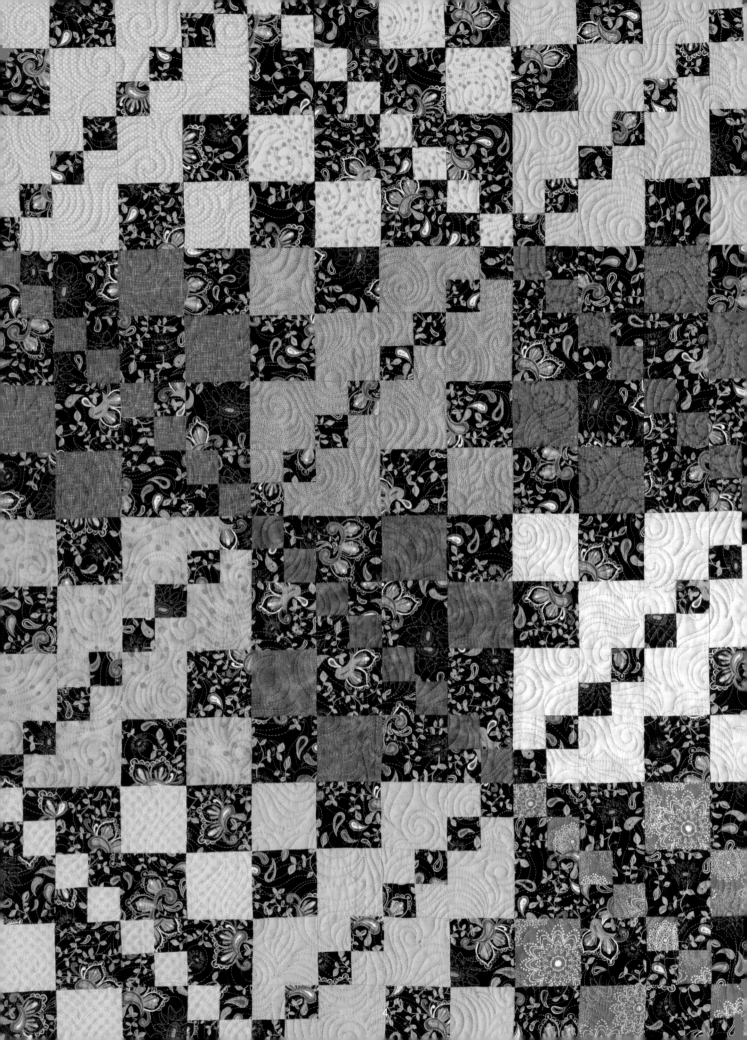

Introduction

Who among us hasn't had a shopping incident involving fat quarters? And who could blame us—they're ubiquitous! Displayed in beautiful bundles on shop shelves, tucked neatly in baskets, and prominently displayed in stacks right by the checkout counter, these pretty little bits of fabric tempt us from every corner, and shop owners know we quilters can't resist them! (I have a sewing-room stash to prove it.)

You can treat yourself to just one or two, buy a bundled assortment, or even splurge on one fat quarter of every fabric in a line. No matter how we acquire them, quilters love to collect and use fat quarters. They're often handier to work with than full-length quarter-yard cuts since they allow you to cut wider pieces or even large appliqué shapes. Given their variety, versatility, and irresistible charm, it's no wonder quilters everywhere are attracted to fat quarters.

For all of us who can't seem to get enough of these 18" x 21" pieces of fabric, the quilters at Martingale have put together a collection of 17 quilt patterns especially designed to be stitched from fat quarters. Some projects use just a few fat quarters combined with a coordinating fabric, while others are made exclusively from fat quarters. You'll find designs that are steeped in tradition as well as some that are quite modern. Whatever your taste in fabric or design, you're sure to find quite a few projects here that are worthy of diving into your stash for—or driving to the nearest quilt shop to stock up!

Karen Costello Soltys
Managing Editor

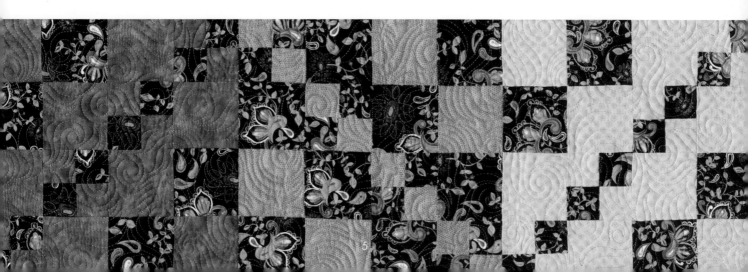

Knockout Roses

Designed, pieced, appliquéd and machine quilted by Nancy Mahoney
Quilt size: 54½" x 54½" | **Block size:** 16" x 16"

MATERIALS

Yardage is based on 42"-wide fabric; fat quarters are 18" x 21".

9 fat quarters of assorted cream prints for block backgrounds and borders

4 fat quarters of assorted tan prints for block backgrounds and border corners

4 fat quarters of assorted red prints for appliqués and inner border

4 fat quarters of assorted black tone-on-tone prints for appliqués and middle borders

4 fat quarters of assorted black-and-cream prints for outer border

2 fat quarters of green prints for leaf and stem appliqués

1 fat quarter of yellow print for appliqués

½ yard of black print for binding

3½ yards of fabric for backing

61" x 61" piece of batting

1¼ yards of lightweight fusible web

³⁄₁₆"-wide fusible tape on a roll (optional)

¼" bias-tape maker

Template plastic

CUTTING

Using the pattern on page 10, make a triangle A template.

From 4 of the cream fat quarters, cut a *total* of:
8 squares, 8½" x 8½"*

1 square, 7¼" x 7¼"; cut into quarters diagonally to yield 4 quarter-square triangles

2 squares, 4⅞" x 4⅞"; cut in half diagonally to yield 4 half-square triangles

4 squares, 3⅞" x 3⅞"; cut in half diagonally to yield 8 half-square triangles

4 squares, 3½" x 3½"

*Cut 2 squares from each cream fat quarter.

From *each* of the tan fat quarters, cut:
2 squares, 8½" x 8½" (8 total)

1 square, 1½" x 1½" (4 total)

From the *bias* of *each* green fat quarter, cut:
16 strips, ½" x 5" (32 total)

A knockout rose is a shrub rose that's hardy and easy to grow, making it a wonderful addition to your garden. These fabric Rose blocks are just as easy to "grow" using fusible machine applique; pieced borders make the quilt a knockout. Your roses will bloom all year long in this stunning quilt.

—Nancy

Continued on page 8

From *each* of the 5 remaining cream fat quarters, cut:

7 of triangle A and 7 of triangle A reversed (70 total; 6 will be left over)

1 square, 7¼" x 7¼" (5 total); cut into quarters diagonally to yield 20 quarter-square triangles

4 strips, 1½" x 10½" (20 total; 4 will be left over)

From *each* of the red fat quarters, cut:

8 of triangle A and 8 of triangle A reversed (64 total)

From *2* of the red fat quarters, cut a *total* of:

2 squares, 4⅞" x 4⅞"; cut in half diagonally to yield 4 half-square triangles

From the black tone-on-tone prints, cut a *total* of:

7 squares, 7¼" x 7¼"; cut into quarters diagonally to yield 28 quarter-square triangles

4 squares, 3½" x 3½"

From *each* of the black-and-cream prints, cut:

4 strips, 3½" x 12½" (16 total)

From the black print, cut:

6 strips, 2¼" x 42"

MAKING THE BLOCKS

1. Sew two different tan 8½" squares and two different cream 8½" squares together as shown to make a Four Patch block. Press the seam allowances as indicated (or press them open to reduce bulk). Make four blocks.

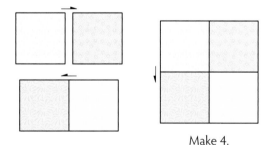

Make 4.

2. To make the stems, place one end of a green bias strip into a ¼" bias-tape maker. Pull the tip of the strip through the bias-tape maker and pin it to your ironing board. Continue to pull the bias-tape maker

slowly along the strip, following close behind it with your iron to crease the edges of the fabric as it emerges from the bias-tape maker. Make 32 bias stems.

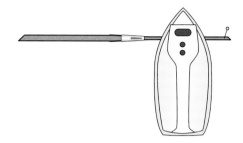

3. With a hot, dry iron, apply a strip of ³⁄₁₆"-wide fusible tape to the back of each bias stem. Applying the tape now will help the strip hold its shape; don't remove the paper backing until you're ready to position the stems on the background.

4. Using the patterns on pages 10–11 and referring to "Fusible Appliqué" on page 89, make the appliqué shapes from the designated fabrics.

5. Using the seam lines as centering lines and working in numerical order, position the shapes on each Four Patch block and appliqué them.

Appliqué placement

MAKING THE INNER BORDER

1. Using a scant ¼" seam allowance, sew the cream and red A triangles together to make a rectangular unit. Press the seam allowances toward the red triangle. The units should measure 2½" x 4½". Make 32 units with the red triangle on the lower

left; label these unit A. Make 32 units with the red triangle on the lower right; label these unit B.

Unit A.   Unit B.
Make 32.   Make 32.

2. Lay out eight A units and eight B units as shown. Using a scant ¼" seam allowance, join the A units to make a 16½"-long strip. If the strip isn't the correct length, adjust the seam allowances accordingly. Press the seam allowances toward the red triangles (or press them open). Repeat to sew the B units together. Then join the strip of A units to the strip of B units to complete the border strip. The border strip should measure 4½" x 32½". Make four border strips.

Make 4.

3. Sew a cream 4⅞" triangle and a red 4⅞" triangle together along their long edges to make a half-square-triangle unit. Press the seam allowances toward the red triangle. Make four and sew them to both ends of two of the border strips from step 2. Press the seam allowances toward the triangle squares.

Make 2.

MAKING THE NARROW AND DOGTOOTH BORDERS

1. Join four cream 1½" x 10½" strips together end to end to make a cream border strip. Press the seam allowances to one side (or press them open). Make four. The border strips should measure 40½" long. Sew tan 1½" squares to both ends of two of the border strips and press the seam allowances toward the cream strips.

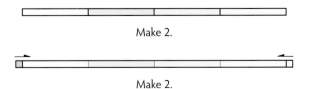

Make 2.

Make 2.

2. Lay out seven black tone-on-tone 7¼" triangles, six cream 7¼" triangles, and two cream 3⅞" triangles as shown. Sew the triangles together using a scant ¼" seam allowance and offsetting the triangles as shown. Press the seam allowances toward the black triangles. Make four dogtooth border strips. The border strips should measure 3½" x 42½". Sew cream 3½" squares to both ends of two of the border strips and press the seam allowances toward the cream squares.

¼"

Make 2.

Make 2.

MAKING THE OUTER BORDER

Sew four black-and-cream strips together end to end. Press the seam allowances to one side (or press them open). Make four outer-border strips. The border strips should measure 3½" x 48½". Sew black tone-on-tone 3½" squares to both ends of two of the border strips and press the seam allowances toward the strips.

Make 2.

Make 2.

ASSEMBLING THE QUILT TOP

1. Lay out the blocks in two rows of two blocks each. Sew the blocks into rows and press the seam allowances in opposite directions from row to row. Then sew the rows together; press the seam allowances in one direction. The quilt top should measure 32½" x 32½".

2. Referring to the layout diagram below, sew the red/cream inner-border strips to the sides, top, and bottom edges of the quilt top. Press the seam allowances toward the quilt center.

3. Sew the narrow cream borders to the sides, top, and bottom edges. Press the seam allowances toward the cream borders.

4. Sew the black/cream dogtooth borders to the sides, top, and bottom edges of the quilt top. Press the seam allowances toward the cream borders.

5. Sew the black outer-border strips to the sides, top, and bottom edges of the quilt top. Press the seam allowances toward the outer borders.

FINISHING THE QUILT

1. Piece and trim the backing to measure approximately 6" larger than the quilt top.

2. Layer the backing, batting, and quilt top; baste. Quilt as desired. The quilt shown was machine quilted in the ditch around the appliqués, with curved lines and loops in the block backgrounds and borders. A wavy line with leaves and swirls was quilted in the outer border.

3. Trim the excess batting and backing even with the quilt top.

4. Use the 2¼"-wide black strips to prepare and attach double-fold binding, referring to "Binding" on page 92. Label your quilt.

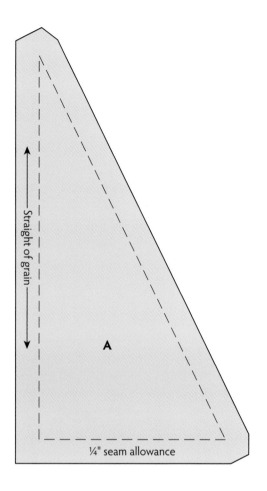

Straight of grain

A

¼" seam allowance

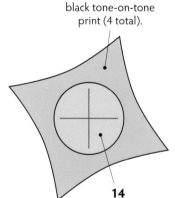

13
Make 1 from each black tone-on-tone print (4 total).

14
Make 1 from each red print (4 total).

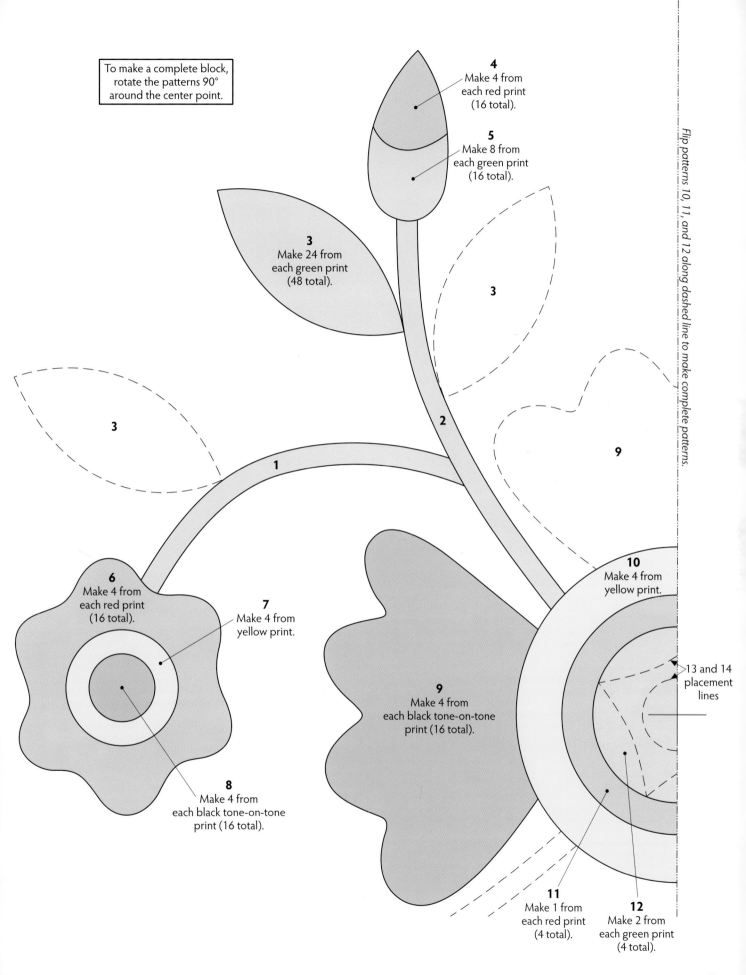

To make a complete block, rotate the patterns 90° around the center point.

4
Make 4 from each red print (16 total).

5
Make 8 from each green print (16 total).

3
Make 24 from each green print (48 total).

3

3

2

1

9

6
Make 4 from each red print (16 total).

7
Make 4 from yellow print.

8
Make 4 from each black tone-on-tone print (16 total).

9
Make 4 from each black tone-on-tone print (16 total).

10
Make 4 from yellow print.

13 and 14 placement lines

11
Make 1 from each red print (4 total).

12
Make 2 from each green print (4 total).

Flip patterns 10, 11, and 12 along dashed line to make complete patterns.

Old Architectural Stars

Designed, pieced, and appliquéd by Karen Costello Soltys; machine quilted by Krista Moser
Quilt size: 75½" x 75½" | **Block size:** 15" x 15"

MATERIALS

Yardage is based on 42"-wide fabric; fat quarters are 18" x 21".

8 to 12 fat quarters of assorted dark reproduction prints (brown, navy blue, medium blue) for pieced blocks*

3 fat quarters of assorted light shirting prints for pieced blocks

3 yards of unbleached muslin for appliqué and pieced blocks

2 yards of red solid for appliqué stars, pieced blocks, and binding**

⅝ yard of cheddar solid for appliqué blocks

2½ yards of 90"-wide fabric for quilt backing***

81" x 81" piece of batting

Template plastic or freezer paper for appliqué template

Fine-point permanent marker

Karen used 10 fat quarters for the quilt shown. Each fat quarter is sufficient to make one and a half blocks. If you don't want to mix the dark fabrics within a block, start with 12 fat quarters.

**If you prefer to cut your binding strips 2½" wide rather than 2", you'll need a total of 2¼ yards of red solid.*

***In keeping with the vintage theme of the quilt, Karen used unbleached muslin for the quilt backing. Using 90"-wide muslin makes a backing without a seam.*

CUTTING

Using the pattern on page 17 and referring to "Making Appliqué Templates" on page 89, make a star template.

From each of the dark fat quarters, cut:
At least 12 squares, 3½" x 3½" (144 total). You need 12 squares per block; if using fewer than 12 fat quarters, cut more squares from each and cobble together renegade blocks from a mix of colors.

From each of the light shirting fat quarters, cut:
20 squares, 3½" x 3½" (60 total)

From the muslin, cut:
13 squares, 10" x 10"

52 rectangles, 3½" x 9½"

48 squares, 3½" x 3½"

From the red solid, cut:
48 squares, 3½" x 3½"

8 binding strips, 2" x 42"*

From the cheddar solid, cut:
5 strips, 3½" x 42"; crosscut into 52 squares, 3½" x 3½"

See "Narrow Binding" on page 16.

I have long loved antique quilts and textiles, and after searching for antique quilt images online, I was inspired to make this rendition modeled after an antique quilt by an unknown Pennsylvanian maker. With just a few slight modifications, I stitched this easy Irish Chain variation. The large muslin blocks are a perfect frame for the stars with holes, which remind me of architectural stars seen on the sides of early homes along the East Coast. The decorative stars were used to cap off steel tie-rods, which were in turn used to stabilize the walls of masonry buildings. Here, as in architecture, the stars are purely decorative, giving a bit of bright red punch to the overall design.

—Karen

PIECING THE 25 PATCH BLOCKS

Instructions are for one block.

1. Choose 12 matching dark 3½" squares. (After you get the hang of it, you can start mixing and matching dark squares, if desired.) You'll also need five matching light-print squares, four muslin 3½" squares, and four red squares. Lay out the squares as shown, with the red squares in the four corners and the muslin squares in the middle position on each edge of the block.

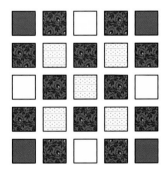

2. Sew the squares together into rows and press the seam allowances toward the dark squares. Sew the rows together and press the seam allowances in one direction. Chain piece (page 87) the squares if you like.

3. Repeat to make 12 blocks that measure 15½", including the outer seam allowances.

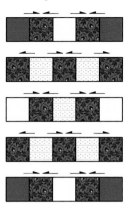 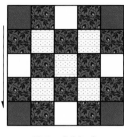

25 Patch block.
Make 12.

MAKING THE APPLIQUÉ BLOCKS

The quilt shown features needle-turn appliqué; if you prefer a faster method, use fusible appliqué. Refer to page 89 for details about either technique.

1. Cut out the center circle in the star template. Trace 13 stars onto the red fabric using a fine-point permanent marker, such as a Pigma pen. Be sure to leave ½" between stars for seam allowances. Cut out the stars roughly ¼" from the marked lines. *Don't cut out the center circle at this time.*

2. Fold a 10" muslin square in half vertically and horizontally and crease to mark placement guidelines. Position a star on the background so that the vertical points align with one fold line and the other fold line intersects the space between the remaining points as shown. Pin the star.

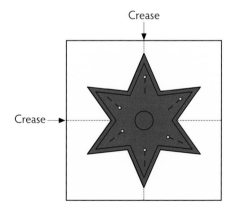

Align top and bottom points
with vertical crease.
Horizontal crease should
intersect star as shown.

3. Use embroidery scissors to snip into the inner corner between two star points so that you can fold under the seam allowance along one edge. Begin appliquéing along that edge.

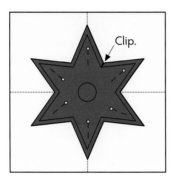

Clip.

4. When you reach the tip of the star point, stitch exactly to the marked point. Take one more tiny stitch at the point to secure, and then fold under the star point as shown. Take another stitch at the point to secure. Then fold the seam allowance the rest of the way under. If necessary, trim the seam allowance to ⅛". (The star points are narrow, so fitting a lot of bulk under them can be difficult unless you trim the seam allowance.)

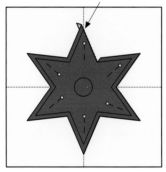

Take extra stitch.

5. Clip into the next inner point so you can easily turn under the second edge of the star point. Continue stitching until you reach the inner point. Take a

second stitch at the innermost point for security, and then sweep under the edge of the adjacent star point to continue stitching.

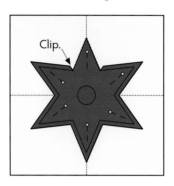

Clip.

6. Repeat steps 4 and 5 until you've worked your way around the entire star. Insert the needle and pull the thread through to the back of the block. Take a few tiny stitches through the muslin, inside the area of the star, to secure; clip the thread.

7. Pull the center of the star away from the muslin so that you can make a snip in it without cutting the muslin. Then slip the tip of your embroidery scissors into the slit and trim the circle approximately ⅛" inside the marked line, leaving a narrow seam allowance. Make small perpendicular snips around the circle so that you'll be able to turn under the edges easily.

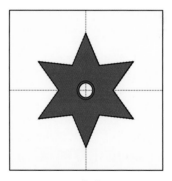

Trim circle, leaving ⅛" seam allowance.

8. Appliqué your way around the circle and fasten off as for the star.

9. Press the star block from the back, and then square up and trim the block to 9½" x 9½", centering the star. (The 4¾" lines on your ruler should run through the center of the star.)

10. Arrange four cheddar squares, four muslin rectangles, and one Star block into three rows. Join the pieces and press the seam allowances as shown. Join the rows. Press the seam allowances away from the center.

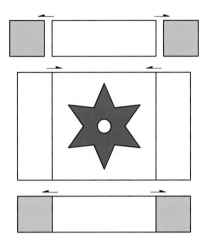

11. Repeat to make a total of 13 Star blocks. The blocks should measure 15½".

ASSEMBLING THE QUILT TOP

1. Starting with a Star block, lay out the Star blocks and pieced blocks in alternating positions to make five rows of five blocks each.

2. Sew the blocks together into rows, pressing the seam allowances away from the Star blocks. Join the rows, pressing the seam allowances in one direction.

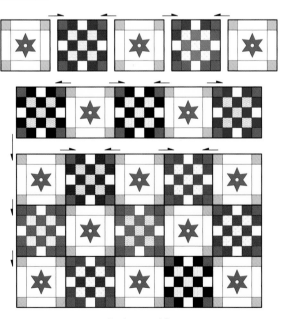

Quilt assembly

FINISHING THE QUILT

1. Trim the backing to measure approximately 6" larger than the quilt top.

2. Layer and baste the backing, batting, and quilt top.

3. Quilt as desired, or deliver your quilt to your favorite professional quilter. The quilt shown was quilted with a crosshatch design in the pieced blocks in keeping with vintage quilting patterns. The appliqué blocks feature a more modern peacock-feather design.

4. Use the red 2"-wide strips to make and attach double-fold binding, referring to "Binding" on page 92.

5. Label and document your quilt so that your quilt, unlike the original inspiration for this quilt, won't later be listed as "maker unknown"!

Narrow Binding

I prefer to cut binding strips 2" wide, rather than the typical 2½". This makes for a binding that is totally filled by the seam allowances of the quilt top, backing, and batting. I feel this narrow binding is in keeping with the binding on many antique quilts, when fabrics were expensive and hard to come by.

—Karen

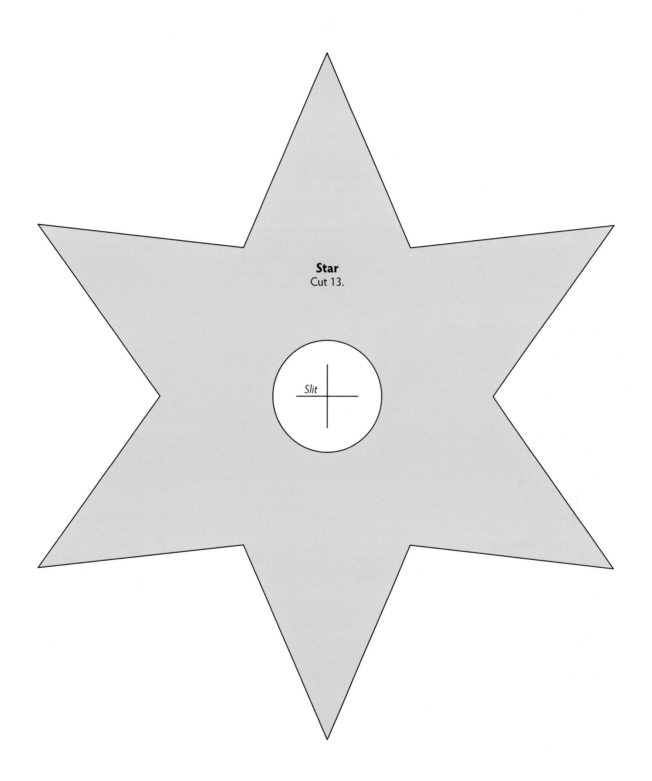

Star
Cut 13.

Slit

Dancing Pinwheels

Designed, pieced, and hand quilted by Virginia Lauth

Quilt size: 36½" x 36½" | **Block sizes: Spiral Pinwheel:** 12" x 12"
Medium Pinwheel: 6" x 6" | **Small Pinwheel:** 3" x 3" | **Pyramid:** 3" x 4"

MATERIALS

Yardage is based on 42"-wide fabric; fat quarters are 18" x 21".

1 yard of white fabric for background

2 fat quarters of yellow prints for blocks

2 fat quarters of dark-blue prints for blocks

1 fat quarter of light-blue print for blocks

⅜ yard of dark-blue print for outer border

⅜ yard of dark-blue print for binding

¼ yard of yellow print for inner border

1¼ yards of fabric for backing

43" x 43" piece of batting

6" x 6" square of template plastic

Blue and yellow fat quarters give this quilt a cheerful, vibrant appeal. For a scrappier effect, choose a greater mix of fat quarters for the four blocks. This quilt size is perfect for a table topper, wall hanging, or baby quilt. You can easily change the color scheme to suit the room in which it will hang or be lovingly used.

—Virginia

A Shortcut to Making Triangle Squares

The following instructions have you cut triangles from squares, and then combine different colored triangles to make units known as triangle squares. I used a nifty technique for making these units by sewing two squares together, and then cutting them apart to yield two finished triangle squares; see page 87.

—Virginia

CUTTING

This quilt is composed of four different blocks made from the same fabrics. As you cut, group the units by block for ease of assembly:

Block A: Spiral Pinwheel

Block B: Medium Pinwheel

Block C: Small Pinwheel

Block D: Pyramid

From the light-blue fat quarter, cut:

2 squares, 4⅞" x 4⅞"; cut in half diagonally to yield 4 half-square triangles (block A)

4 squares, 3⅞" x 3⅞"; cut in half diagonally to yield 8 half-square triangles (block B)

Continued on page 20

From the yellow fat quarters, cut:

1 square, 5¼" x 5¼"; cut into quarters diagonally to yield 4 quarter-square triangles (block A)

2 squares, 4⅞" x 4⅞"; cut in half diagonally to yield 4 half-square triangles (block A)

4 rectangles, 3½" x 4½" (block D)

24 squares, 2⅜" x 2⅜"; cut in half diagonally to yield 48 half-square triangles (block C)

From the dark-blue fat quarters, cut:

1 square, 5¼" x 5¼"; cut into quarters diagonally to yield 4 quarter-square triangles (block A)

4 squares, 3⅞" x 3⅞"; cut in half diagonally to yield 8 half-square triangles (block B)

24 squares, 2⅜" x 2⅜"; cut in half diagonally to yield 48 half-square triangles (block C)

From the white fabric, cut:

2 squares, 4⅞" x 4⅞"; cut in half diagonally to yield 4 half-square triangles (block A)

8 rectangles, 3½" x 4½"

1 square, 4½" x 4½" (block A)

8 squares, 3⅞" x 3⅞"; cut in half diagonally to yield 16 half-square triangles (block B)

28 squares, 3½" x 3½" (background)

4 rectangles, 2¾" x 4" (block D)

48 squares, 2⅜" x 2⅜"; cut in half diagonally to yield 96 half-square triangles (block C)

From the yellow print, cut:

4 strips, 1½" x 42"

From the dark-blue print for outer border, cut:

4 strips, 2½" x 42"

From the dark-blue print for binding, cut:

4 strips, 2½" x 42"

Easy Organization

There are many sizes of triangles in this project. To keep things simple, they are identified by the size of the square from which they were originally cut.

–Virginia

PIECING THE BLOCKS
Block A: Spiral Pinwheel

1. Sew a yellow 5¼" triangle and a dark-blue 5¼" triangle together. Press the seam allowances toward the dark-blue fabric. Repeat to make a total of four triangle units.

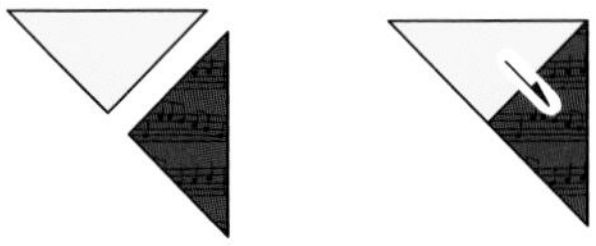

Make 4.

2. Sew a pieced triangle from step 1 and a light-blue 4⅞" triangle together. Press the seam allowances toward the light-blue triangle. Repeat to make a total of four pieced squares.

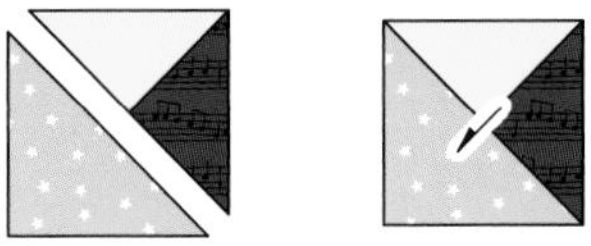

Make 4.

3. Sew a white 4⅞" triangle and a yellow 4⅞" triangle together. Press the seam allowances toward the white triangle. Repeat to make a total of four triangle squares.

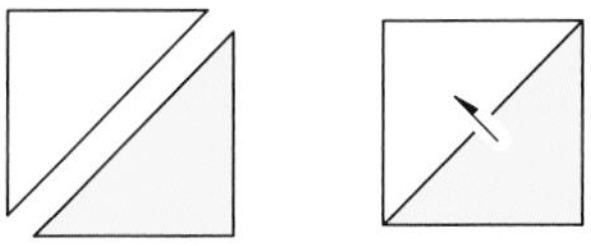

Make 4.

4. Sew the units from steps 2 and 3 together into rows as shown, adding the white 4½" square to the center. Press the seam allowances in opposite directions from row to row. Join the rows. Press the seam allowances in the same direction to complete block A.

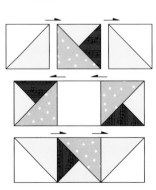 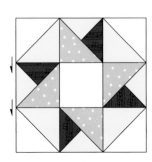

Block A.
Make 1.

Block B: Medium Pinwheel

1. Sew a white 3⅞" triangle and a light-blue 3⅞" triangle together as shown. Press the seam allowances toward the light-blue fabric. Make two units.

Make 2.

2. Repeat with white and dark-blue 3⅞" triangles. Make two units.

Make 2.

3. Sew the triangle squares together to make two rows. Press the seam allowances in opposite directions from row to row. Join the rows. Press the seam allowances in the same direction. Make four of block B.

Block B.
Make 4.

Block C: Small Pinwheel

You'll make 20 small Pinwheel blocks with the blades rotating counterclockwise and four small Pinwheel blocks with the blades rotating clockwise.

1. Sew a white 2⅜" triangle and a yellow 2⅜" triangle together as shown. Press the seam allowances toward the yellow fabric. Make two units. Repeat with white and dark-blue 2⅜" triangles. Press the seam allowances toward the dark-blue fabric. Make two units.

Make 2.   Make 2.

2. Sew the triangle squares together to make two rows. Press the seam allowances in opposite directions from row to row. Join the rows. Press the seam allowances in the same direction. Make 20 small Pinwheel blocks with the blades rotating counterclockwise.

Block C.
Make 20 counterclockwise.

3. Paying careful attention to the orientation of the pieces, make four small Pinwheel blocks with the blades rotating clockwise.

Block C.
Make 4 clockwise.

Block D: Pyramid

1. Using the pattern on page 23, make a pyramid D template. Cut four pyramid triangles from the yellow 3½" x 4½" rectangles.

2. Cut the white 2¾" x 4" rectangles diagonally as shown to create four left triangles and four right triangles.

Left triangle.   Right triangle.
Cut 4.   Cut 4.

3. Sew a left triangle to a pyramid triangle as shown. Press the seam allowances toward the white triangle. Repeat on the opposite edge with a right triangle. Make four of block D.

Block D.
Make 4.

ASSEMBLING THE UNITS

To ease construction of the quilt top, assemble the appropriate blocks into the following units. Pay careful attention to the color placement and rotation of the small Pinwheel blocks.

Pyramid Unit

Join white 3½" x 4½" rectangles to both sides of a yellow Pyramid block. Press the seam allowances toward the white rectangles. Repeat to make a total of four units.

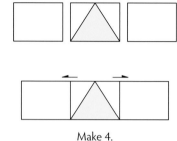

Make 4.

Small Pinwheel Block Unit

1. Sew a white 3½" square to a counterclockwise Pinwheel block. Repeat to make two additional units using counterclockwise Pinwheel blocks and white squares, carefully orienting the Pinwheel blocks. For the fourth unit, join a white square to a *clockwise* Pinwheel block. Press the seam allowances as shown. Join the units to make one large unit. Press the seam allowances in one direction. Make a total of four units.

Clockwise block

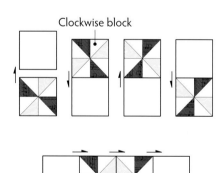

Make 4.

2. Attach a pyramid unit to a pinwheel unit made in step 1. Repeat to make a total of four units.

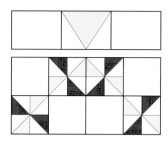

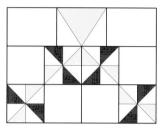

Make 4.

Corner Units

1. Sew white 3½" squares to the sides of a small Pinwheel block as shown. Press the seam allowances toward the white squares.

2. Sew a white square to the bottom edge of a small Pinwheel block. Press the seam allowances toward the white square. Sew this unit to the left side of a medium Pinwheel block. Press the seam allowances toward the medium Pinwheel block. Join the two rows to make one corner unit. Repeat to make a total of four corner units.

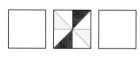

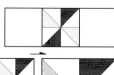
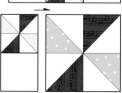

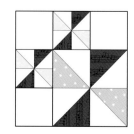

Make 4.

ASSEMBLING THE QUILT TOP

Refer to the illustration to arrange and join the units and block A into rows. Press the seam allowances in opposite directions from row to row. Join the rows. Press the seam allowances in the same direction. The quilt top should measure 30½" x 30½".

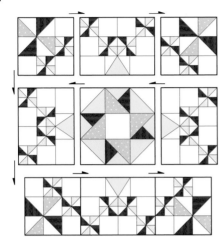

ADDING THE BORDERS

1. Trim two yellow strips to 30½" and attach to the sides of the quilt top. Press the seam allowances toward the borders. Trim the remaining strips to 32½" and attach to the top and bottom. Press the seam allowances toward the borders.

2. Trim two dark-blue strips to 32½" and attach to the sides of the quilt top. Press the seam allowances toward the dark-blue borders. Trim the remaining strips to 36½" and attach to the top and bottom. Press the seam allowances toward the dark-blue borders.

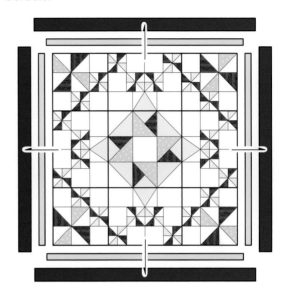

FINISHING THE QUILT

1. Piece and trim the backing to measure approximately 6" larger than the quilt top.

2. Layer the backing, batting, and quilt top; baste. Quilt as desired.

3. Trim the excess batting and backing even with the quilt top.

4. Use the 2½"-wide dark-blue strips to prepare and attach double-fold binding, referring to "Binding" on page 92. Label your quilt.

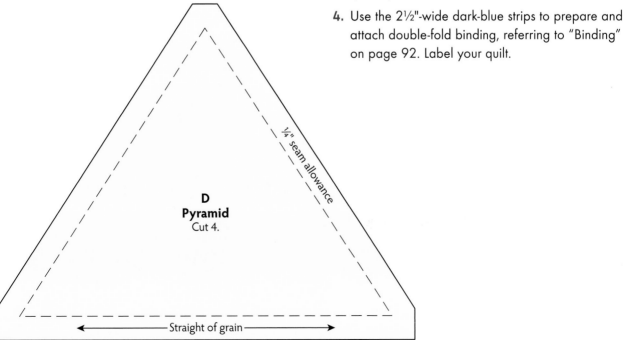

D
Pyramid
Cut 4.

¼" seam allowance

←———— Straight of grain ————→

Ray of Light

Designed and pieced by Regina Girard; machine quilted by Karen Burns of Compulsive Quilting

Quilt size: 50½" x 60½" | **Block size:** 10" x 10"

MATERIALS

Yardage is based on 42"-wide fabric; fat quarters are 18" x 21".

5 dark fat quarters (1 each of blue, purple, black, red, and orange) for blocks*

5 light fat quarters (1 each of yellow, pink, light blue, light orange, and gray) for blocks*

1⅞ yards of dark batik for border and binding

3½ yards of fabric or flannel for backing

57" x 67" piece of batting

6" x 6" square of template plastic

If you don't have at least 21" of usable fabric across each fat quarter, you'll need two of each color.

CUTTING

Separate your fat quarters into pairs of one light and one dark fabric and keep them together as you cut the pieces. Refer to the cutting diagram below.

From *each* fat quarter, cut:

1 strip, 5½" x 21"; crosscut into 3 rectangles, 5½" x 6½"

2 strips, 3" x 21"; crosscut each strip into 3 rectangles, 3" x 4" (6 total), and 3 squares, 3" x 3" (6 total)

1 strip, 5½" x 21"; crosscut into 1 rectangle, 5½" x 6½". Trim the remaining strip to 3" wide, and cut:

    2 rectangles, 3" x 4"

    2 squares, 3" x 3"

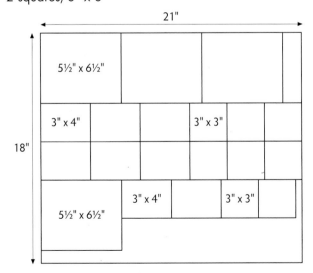

From the *lengthwise grain* of the dark batik, cut:

4 strips, 5½" x 50½"

5 strips, 2½" x 54"

I love these light-value batik fabrics—they really glow. The juxtaposition of the lights and darks establishes the pattern in this quilt and creates a sense of movement. The design may look difficult, but Sally Schneider's easy method for making shaded four-patch units speeds up the assembly process. And, you don't need to cut any triangles, which is always a bonus in my book.

—Regina

PIECING THE BLOCK UNITS

You'll make two different pieced units, A and B, with the lights and darks reversed between them.

Unit A   Unit B

Unit A

1. Working with the pieces you cut from each pair of light and dark fat quarters, gather the light 3" squares, the dark 3" x 4" rectangles, and the light 5½" x 6½" rectangles.

2. Sew a light 3" square to the end of each dark 3" x 4" rectangle. Press the seam allowances toward the rectangles. Make two units.

Make 2.

3. Sew the rectangle units together as shown, carefully matching the outside edges.

4. Clip through the seam allowances in the middle of the unit. Don't worry if you clip through the stitching; you'll cut the units diagonally through the middle in step 8. Open the unit and press the seam allowances toward the dark rectangles, changing the pressing direction at the clip.

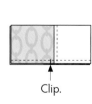

Clip.

5. Cut the template plastic into a 5½" square; cut the square in half diagonally to make a template for marking sewing lines on the units.

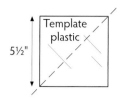

6. Align the corner and left edge of the template with the corner and left edge of the sewn rectangle as shown. Draw a diagonal line, making sure the line goes from the corner of the sewn rectangle and passes a few threads beyond the corner of the square at the block center. You may need to switch marking pencils for your light and dark fabrics. Flip the block and mark the stitching line on the opposite side as well.

7. With right sides together, pin a light 5½" x 6½" rectangle to the pieced unit.

Pin Why?

I freely admit that I am an obsessive pinner; if I don't pin, fabric tends to slide around. To prevent the top and bottom fabrics from stretching when you sew on the marked lines, pin the pieces securely.

—Regina

8. Sew on each diagonal marked line, starting on the side of the rectangle, not the point. (Your machine may eat the fabric if you start on the point.) Cut between the sewing lines with your rotary cutter to make two units.

 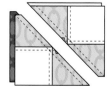

9. Open the units and press the seam allowances toward the pieced triangles. Repeat to make a total of eight A units using these pieces. Make a total of 40 A units.

Unit A.
Make 8.

Unit B

1. Working with the same color combination as your first group of A units, gather the dark 3" squares, the light 3" x 4" rectangles, and the dark 5½" x 6½" rectangles.

2. Sew a dark 3" square to the end of each light 3" x 4" rectangle. Press the seam allowances toward the squares. Make two units.

Make 2.

3. Sew two of these rectangle units together, carefully matching the outside edges.

4. Clip through the seam allowance in the middle of the unit. Open the unit and press the seam allowances toward the dark squares, changing the pressing direction at the clip.

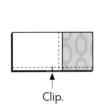 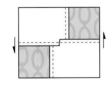

Clip.

5. Repeat the marking, sewing, and cutting process as for the A units, combining the pieced unit with a dark 5½" x 6½" rectangle. Make a total of eight B units using these pieces.

Unit B.
Make 8.

6. Using the pieces cut from the remaining fat quarters, make a total of 40 B units.

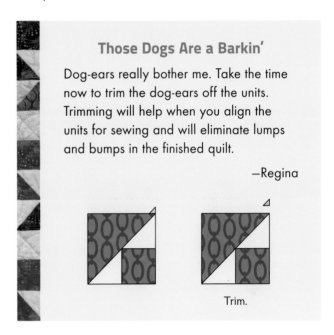

Those Dogs Are a Barkin'

Dog-ears really bother me. Take the time now to trim the dog-ears off the units. Trimming will help when you align the units for sewing and will eliminate lumps and bumps in the finished quilt.

—Regina

Trim.

ASSEMBLING THE BLOCKS

1. Arrange the A and B units on your design wall as shown on page 28, distributing the color and pattern evenly before sewing the units into blocks. (If you prefer a more random color placement, sew the units into blocks first, and then arrange the blocks.)

2. To make each block, sew the top units together. Press the seam allowances toward the B unit. Repeat with the bottom units. Join the rows. Press

the seam allowances up or down, alternating the direction from block to block. Repeat to make 20 blocks.

Again with the Pinning

The seam allowances will "nest" nicely, making it easy to sew the blocks together. Still, I recommend that you pin the seam intersections before sewing so they'll match.

—Regina

ASSEMBLING THE QUILT TOP

Sew the blocks together into rows. Press the seam allowances in opposite directions from row to row. Join the rows. Press the seam allowances in the same direction. The quilt top should measure 40½" x 50½".

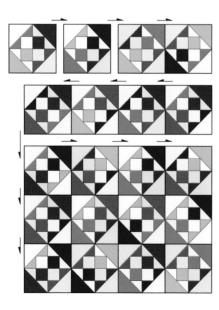

ADDING THE BORDER

1. Sew 5½" x 50½" border strips to the sides of the quilt top. Press the seam allowances toward the border strips.

2. Repeat with the remaining border strips at the top and bottom of the quilt top.

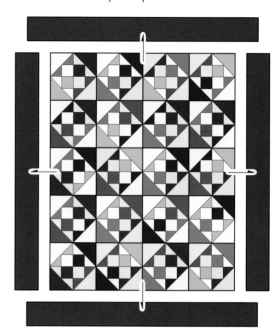

FINISHING THE QUILT

1. Piece and trim the backing to measure approximately 6" larger than the quilt top.

2. Layer the backing, batting, and quilt top; baste. Quilt as desired or deliver your quilt to your favorite professional quilter. Regina's quilt was machine quilted in diagonal lines through the block centers and with alternating large and small circles.

3. Trim the excess batting and backing even with the quilt top.

4. Use the 2½"-wide dark-batik strips to make and attach double-fold binding, referring to "Binding" on page 92. Label your quilt.

Shakespeare in Leaves

Designed and pieced by Mary J. Burns; machine quilted by Karen Burns of Compulsive Quilting

Quilt size: 68½" x 78½" | **Block size:** 12" x 18"

The Pacific Northwest is blessed with wonderful autumn weather, and crisp winds blow away our usual gray clouds to reveal beautiful blue skies. I love deciduous trees, and am poetically inspired by the numerous shades the leaves turn in the fall—something I tried to reflect in this Maple Leaf quilt. You can almost see the blue pinwheels on this quilt spinning in the wind!

—Mary

MATERIALS

Yardage is based on 42"-wide fabric; fat quarters are 18" x 21".

1 fat quarter *each* of 2 different light-blue prints for Pinwheel blocks

1 fat quarter *each* of 2 different dark-blue prints for Pinwheel blocks

2 fat quarters of red prints for Maple Leaf blocks

1 fat quarter *each* of yellow, orange, lime-green, and black prints for Maple Leaf blocks (for a scrappier look, use 12 different prints for leaves)

3 yards of dark-gray print for sashing strips and binding

1½ yards of sky-blue print for block backgrounds

4¾ yards of fabric for backing

74" x 84" piece of batting

CUTTING

See *"Cutting Fat Quarters"* on page 87.

From *each* of the light-blue and dark-blue fat quarters, cut:
5 strips, 3¼" x 21"; crosscut into 20 rectangles, 3¼" x 4½" (80 total)

From *each* of the red, yellow, orange, lime-green, and black fat quarters, cut:
1 strip, 9¼" x 18"; crosscut into 1 rectangle, 9¼" x 13¼", and 2 rectangles, 1½" x 9¼"

2 strips, 5¼" x 18"; crosscut into 4 rectangles, 5¼" x 7½"

From the sky-blue print, cut:
2 strips, 4½" x 42"; crosscut into 12 rectangles, 4½" x 6½"

From the remaining sky-blue print, cut on the *lengthwise* grain:
2 strips, 9¼" wide; crosscut into 6 rectangles, 9¼" x 13¼"

3 strips, 7½" wide; crosscut into 24 rectangles, 5¼" x 7½"

From the dark-gray print, cut:
6 strips, 6½" x 42"; crosscut into 16 rectangles, 6½" x 12½"

2 strips, 18½" x 42"; crosscut into 15 rectangles, 4½" x 18½"

8 strips, 2½" x 42"

Cutting Triangles from Rectangles

Unlike squares cut diagonally, triangles cut from rectangles are not identical regardless of the direction you cut. Carefully follow the instructions for cutting all rectangles to ensure that your blocks turn out as planned.

—Mary

PIECING THE PINWHEEL BLOCKS

1. Make four stacks of light-blue 3¼" x 4½" rectangles, with 10 rectangles in each stack. Working with only four pieces at a time, cut the rectangles in the first two stacks in half diagonally in one direction. Label these as A triangles. Cut the rectangles in the remaining two stacks in half diagonally in the opposite direction and label these as A reversed triangles (AR). You'll have 40 of each.

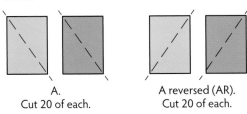

A.
Cut 20 of each.

A reversed (AR).
Cut 20 of each.

2. Stack and cut the dark-blue 3¼" x 4½" rectangles in the same way to yield 40 dark-blue B triangles and 40 dark-blue B reversed triangles (BR).

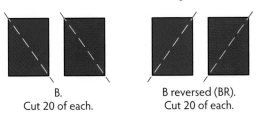

B.
Cut 20 of each.

B reversed (BR).
Cut 20 of each.

To Pin or Not to Pin?

That is the question. I sew carefully with scant ¼" seam allowances; if you do this, and because these units will be trimmed to size, it's all right not to pin them. Be careful not to stretch the bias edges as you sew the triangles; a walking foot is very helpful.

—Mary

3. Sew a light-blue A triangle and a dark-blue B triangle together, matching the end points along the longest edges of the triangles as shown. Sew the triangles together using a scant ¼" seam allowance. Chain piece (page 87) the remaining A and B triangles for efficiency. Press the seam

allowances toward the dark-blue fabric. Make a total of 40 pieced rectangle units.

Make 20 of each.

4. In the same manner, sew a light-blue AR triangle and a dark-blue BR triangle together. Press the seam allowances toward the dark-blue fabric. Make a total of 40 pieced rectangle units.

Make 20 of each.

5. To trim the pinwheel units, set the 2½" ruler mark on the seam at one corner, with the 3½" ruler mark on the seam at the opposite corner. Trim ⅛" to ¼" off the two edges. Then rotate the unit (or your ruler) and line up the clean-cut edges with the 2½" and 3½" ruler marks and trim the remaining two sides. Each trimmed rectangle should measure 2½" x 3½".

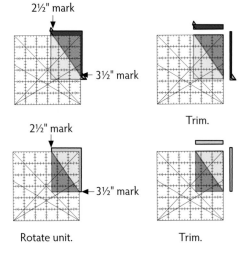

2½" mark

3½" mark

Trim.

2½" mark

3½" mark

Rotate unit.

Trim.

6. Arrange each Pinwheel block using two A/B units and two AR/BR units; 10 blocks will "spin" to the right and 10 blocks will "spin" to the left. Sew the units together in rows. Press the seam allowances open to reduce the bulk. Join the rows. I use one pin when joining the rows, sticking the pin all the way through both pieces at the center intersection of the

points. Press the seam allowances open. Make 10 of each Pinwheel block.

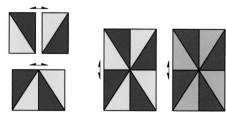

Make 10 of each.

PIECING THE MAPLE LEAF BLOCKS

1. For both the colored leaf fabrics *and* the sky-blue fabric, cut the 5¼" x 7½" rectangles in half diagonally, from *top right* to *bottom left*, right side up, as shown. Cut the 9¼" x 13¼" rectangles in half diagonally in the opposite direction, from *top left* to *bottom right*, right side facing up.

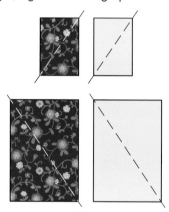

2. Sew each small leaf print triangle and a small sky-blue triangle together, matching the end points along the longest edges of the triangles. Chain piece the units using a scant ¼" seam allowance. Press the seam allowances toward the sky fabric. Make four rectangle units from each fat quarter for a total of 48 small leaf/sky rectangles.

Make 48.

3. As you did with the Pinwheel blocks, trim the rectangle units, this time aligning the 4½" and 6½" marks with the diagonal seam. The trimmed units should measure 4½" x 6½".

4. To make each leaf stem using the 1½" x 9¼" rectangles, see "Making Bias Stems" on page 90. The finished stems will measure approximately ½" wide.

The Bridge Is the Thing

Because these long, skinny triangle tips have a tendency to get tangled in with your bobbin thread when sewing, use a bridge—a square scrap of fabric with which you always start and end your chain sewing. Sewing on the square first creates enough thread tension to feed the triangle tips safely without having the feed dogs eat them. Ending a chain with a bridge sets you up for the next chain.

—Mary

5. Pin or glue baste one end of the stem perpendicular to the diagonal edge of a large sky triangle, centering the stem along the edge. Pin or glue baste the free end of the stem to the sky triangle 1¼" from the corner. Machine appliqué the stem to the block in a gentle curve using a narrow zigzag stitch and matching thread. Stitch the inside of the curve first, and then sew the outside edge.

6. Sew a large leaf triangle and a large sky triangle together, matching the end points along the diagonal edges of the triangles and sandwiching the stem between the layers. Carefully press the seam allowances toward the leaf fabric. Make two units from each fat quarter for a total of 12 large leaf/sky rectangles.

1¼"

7. Trim the units, this time aligning the 8½" and 12½" marks with the diagonal seam. The trimmed units should measure 8½" x 12½".

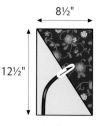

8½"

12½"

Make 12.

8. To assemble each Maple Leaf block, sew two small leaf/sky rectangle units to one 4½" x 6½" sky rectangle as shown. Press the seam allowances toward the sky rectangle.

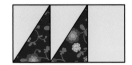

9. Sew two small leaf/sky rectangle units end to end as shown. Press the seam allowances downward.

10. Sew the unit from the previous step to the right edge of the large leaf rectangle. Press the seam allowances toward the large rectangle. Add the unit made in step 8 to the top. Press the seam allowances toward the large rectangle. The block should measure 12½" x 18½". Make 12 Maple Leaf blocks.

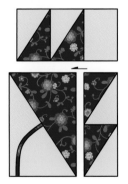 

Make 12.

ASSEMBLING THE QUILT TOP

1. Referring to the illustration at right, arrange the Maple Leaf blocks and dark-gray 4½" x 18½" sashing strips in three horizontal rows of four blocks each. Sew a sashing strip between the blocks and to the left and right ends of each row. Press the seam allowances toward the sashing strips. The rows should measure 68½" long.

2. Sew the Pinwheel blocks and the dark-gray 6½" x 12½" sashing strips into four horizontal rows, alternating the direction the pinwheels spin from row to row. (Sew with the Pinwheel blocks on top to intersect the points precisely and avoid catching the seam allowances.) Press the seam allowances toward the sashing strips. The rows should measure 68½" long.

3. Join the rows, paying attention to the direction the pinwheels spin and matching the block intersections. Press the seam allowances in one direction.

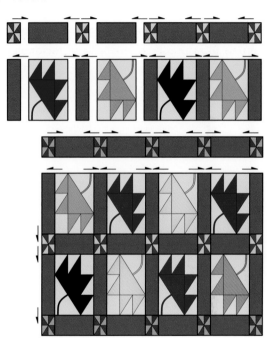

FINISHING THE QUILT

1. Piece and trim the backing to measure approximately 6" larger than the quilt top.

2. Layer the backing, batting, and quilt top; baste. Quilt as desired. Karen quilted veins in the big maple leaves in variegated-green thread, a swirl design in the light-blue background, and leaves on a vine in the dark-gray sashing.

3. Trim the excess batting and backing even with the quilt top.

4. Use the 2½"-wide dark-gray strips to prepare and attach double-fold binding, referring to "Binding" on page 92. Label your quilt.

Heat Wave

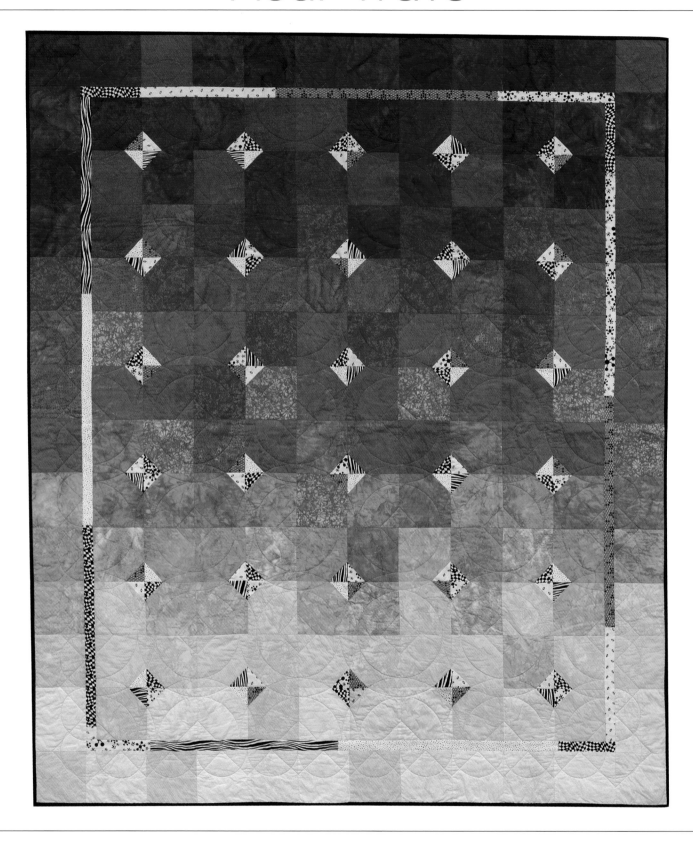

Designed, pieced, and machine quilted by Abbi Barden; quilting motif by Lorraine Torrence

Quilt size: 62½" x 72½" | **Block size:** 10" x 10"

MATERIALS

Yardage is based on 42"-wide fabric; fat quarters are 18" x 21".

20 fat quarters of red, red-orange, orange, yellow-orange, and yellow batiks in textured solids and tone-on-tone prints for blocks and outer border

6 fat quarters of black-and-white prints for blocks and inner border

⅝ yard of black fabric for binding

3¾ yards of fabric for backing (crosswise seam)

69" x 79" piece of batting

CUTTING

From *each* of the 2 darkest red fat quarters and the 2 lightest yellow fat quarters, cut:
2 rectangles, 5½" x 6½" (8 total)

From *all* of the analogous fat quarters, cut a *total* of:
160 squares, 5½" x 5½"

From *each* black-and-white fat quarter, cut:
2 strips, 1½" x 21" (12 total)
20 squares, 2⅜" x 2⅜" (120 total)

From the black fabric, cut:
7 strips, 2½" x 42"

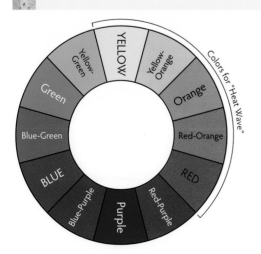

Color Flow

Before assembling the blocks, arrange the colored pieces on a design wall or other flat surface, including the outer-border squares and rectangles, until you're pleased with the flow of the colors from one piece to the next.

—Abbi

I designed this quilt using a palette of colors that lie next to each other on the color wheel, known as an analogous combination. Five warm colors—red, red-orange, orange, yellow-orange, and yellow—provide the "heat." Black-and-white scrappy diamonds create the surface pattern. To make this quilt in different colors, choose a color on the wheel and count in either direction for three to five colors. For example, you can use blue-purple, blue, blue-green, green, and yellow-green for a cooler scheme. Purple, red-purple, red, red-orange, and orange also work.

—Abbi

PIECING THE BLOCKS

1. Referring to "Folded Corners" on page 88, sew a 2⅜" black-and-white square to each of the four 5½" colored squares that will be the upper-left corner block of the quilt interior. Press the seam allowances outward on diagonally opposing squares and inward on the remaining squares.

2. Sew the four folded-corner units together into a block. Working across the top row, make a total of five blocks, alternating the pressing direction of the horizontal seam allowances from block to block as shown.

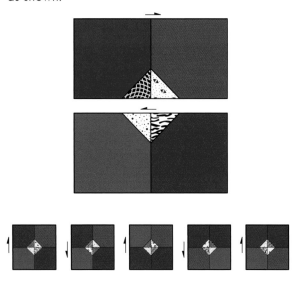

3. Repeat to make a total of 30 blocks.

ASSEMBLING THE QUILT TOP

Arrange the blocks in six horizontal rows of five blocks each. Sew the blocks together in rows. Press the seam allowances in opposite directions from row to row. Join the rows. Press the seam allowances in one direction. The quilt top should measure 50½" x 60½".

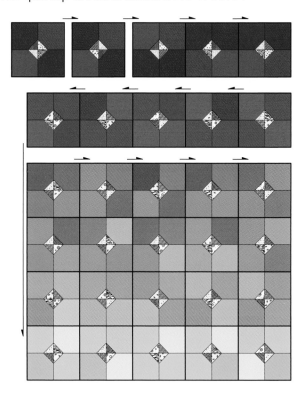

ADDING THE BORDERS

1. Stitch the 1½" black-and-white strips together end to end in random order to make one long strip. Cut two strips, 60½" long, and attach them to the sides of the quilt top. Press the seam allowances toward the inner borders. Cut two strips, 52½" long, and attach them to the top and bottom. Press the seam allowances toward the borders.

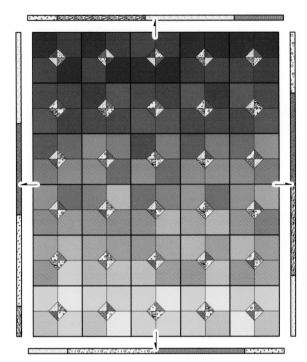

2. For the top outer border, join eight 5½" squares and add a 5½" x 6½" rectangle (marked with a "R" in the illustration) at each end as shown. The border should measure 52½" long. Repeat for the bottom outer border. Attach the top and bottom borders to the quilt top. Press the seam allowances toward the inner borders.

3. For each side border, join two 5½" x 6½" rectangles (marked with an "R" in the illustration) and 12 squares, with one square at each end as shown. These borders should measure 72½" long. Attach the side borders. Press the seam allowances toward the inner borders.

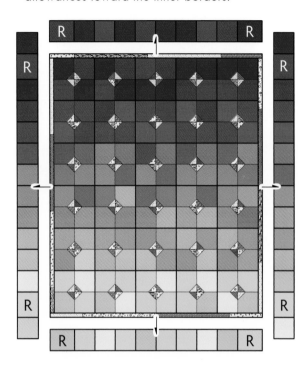

FINISHING THE QUILT

1. Piece and trim the backing to measure approximately 6" larger than the quilt top.

2. Layer the backing, batting, and quilt top; baste. Quilt as desired.

3. Trim the excess batting and backing even with the quilt top.

4. Use the 2½"-wide black strips to make and attach double-fold binding, referring to "Binding" on page 92. Label your quilt.

Sherbet Punch

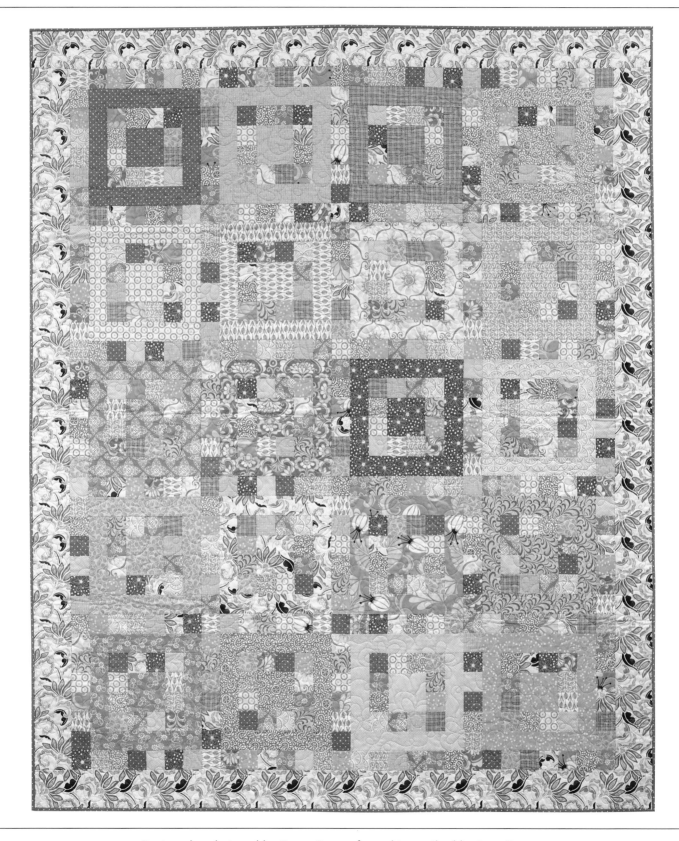

Designed and pieced by Tracy Overturf; machine quilted by Lynn Reppas

Quilt size: 66½" x 80½" | **Block size:** 12" x 12"

MATERIALS

Yardage is based on 42"-wide fabric; fat quarters are 18" x 21".

20 fat quarters for blocks and sashing*

1⅛ yards of fabric for border

⅔ yard of fabric for binding

5 yards of fabric for backing

73" x 87" piece of batting

Don't prewash the fabrics in this case; you'll need the full size of the unwashed fat quarters to cut the pieces needed.

CUTTING

From *each* fat quarter, cut:
1 strip, 5" x 21"; from each strip, cut 1 square, 4½" x 4½" (20 total). Cut the remainder of the strip lengthwise into 2 strips, 2½" wide. From each strip cut 1 rectangle, 2½" x 12½" (40 total), and 1 square, 2½" x 2½" (40 total).

1 strip, 2½" x 21"; crosscut into 2 rectangles, 2½" x 8½" (40 total), and 1 square, 2½" x 2½" (20 total)

4 strips, 2½" x 21" (80 total; 4 will be left over)

From the border fabric, cut:
8 strips, 4½" x 42"

From the binding fabric, cut:
8 strips, 2½" x 42"

PIECING THE BLOCKS

1. Sew two 2½" x 21" assorted strips together to make a strip set; repeat to make a total of 10 strip sets. Press the seam allowances toward the darker fabric in each set. Cut each strip set into eight units, 2½" x 4½", for a total of 80 units.

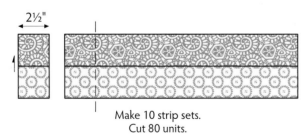

2½"

Make 10 strip sets.
Cut 80 units.

Collecting the fat quarters for this quilt is half the fun, especially if you do it a little at a time. Just pick a color scheme and look for those colors at each quilt shop you visit. When you look at the finished quilt, you'll remember where you got each fabric!

—Tracy

2. Sew units from step 1 to opposite sides of a 4½" square, making sure to use different-colored units. Press the seam allowances toward the center square. Make 20.

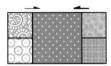

Make 20.

3. From the remaining 2½" x 21" strips, create five groups of four strips each, making sure to use four different fabrics in each set. Sew the strips in each set together and press the outer seam allowances outward and the inner seam allowances in either direction. Cut each strip set into eight units, 2½" x 8½", for a total of 40 units.

Make 5 strip sets.
Cut 40 units.

4. Sew units from step 3 to the remaining sides of each unit from step 2, making sure to vary the fabrics. Press the seam allowances toward the top and bottom units.

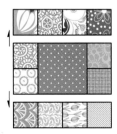

5. Sew 2½" x 8½" rectangles that match the center square to opposite sides of each block. Press the seam allowances toward the rectangles. Sew matching 2½" x 12½" rectangles to the top and bottom of each block. Press the seam allowances toward the rectangles. The blocks should measure 12½" x 12½".

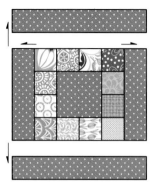

Make 20.

6. For the sashing, make six strip sets of six assorted 2½" x 21" strips each. Cut each strip set into eight units, 2½" x 12½", for a total of 48 units. Press the seam allowances on each end inward and the remaining seam allowances in either direction.

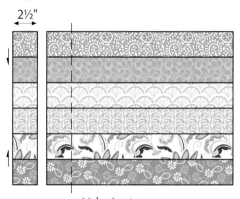

Make 6 strip sets.
Cut 48 units.

Not Enough Variety in Your Sashing?

I don't like it when pieces of the same fabric touch, so I go out of my way to avoid that—including unsewing if necessary. You can take units apart and recombine the pieces to make new units, or make new sets by using pairs or singles. You'll have enough extra segments to allow you to keep squares of the same fabric from being too close together.

—Tracy

ASSEMBLING THE QUILT TOP

1. Arrange the blocks and sashing strips into a horizontal row as shown. Sew one sashing strip to the left side of each block and to the left and right sides of the last block in the row. Press the seam allowances toward the blocks. Sew the blocks and their sashing strips together. Press the seam allowances toward the blocks. Make five rows.

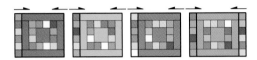

Make 5.

2. Randomly sew leftover strip sets of six and two squares, along with single squares, into six sashing strips of 29 pieces each.

Make 6.

3. Sew the sashing strips to the top of each row and to the top and bottom of the last row. Join the rows. Press the seam allowances toward the block rows.

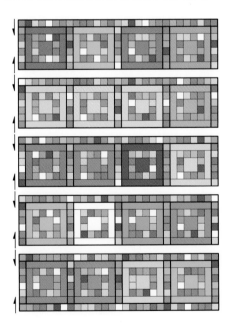

ADDING THE BORDER

1. Sew two 4½" x 42" strips together; repeat to make four long strips. From those strips, cut two 72½"-long strips and sew them to the sides of the quilt top. Press the seam allowances toward the borders.

2. Cut two 66½"-long strips and sew them to the top and bottom of the quilt top. Press the seam allowances toward the borders.

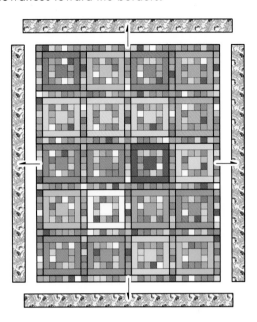

FINISHING THE QUILT

1. Piece and trim the backing to measure approximately 6" larger than the quilt top.

2. Layer the backing, batting, and quilt top; baste. Quilt as desired. Tracy's quilt was machine quilted in an allover freehand design of flowers and swirls.

3. Trim the excess batting and backing even with the quilt top.

4. Use the 2½"-wide strips to make and attach double-fold binding, referring to "Binding" on page 92. Label your quilt.

Want a Simpler Look?

Try making the quilt with all the 8½" and 12½" strips and center squares cut from just one fabric, and then put the variety in the strip sets and pairs. This gives you a completely different look from the same pattern.

—Tracy

Nā Kai O Kaua'i: The Waters of Kaua'i

Designed and pieced by Leanne Clare; machine quilted by Karen Burns of Compulsive Quilting

Quilt size: 64½" x 64½" | **Block size:** 8" x 8"

MATERIALS

Yardage is based on 42"-wide fabric; fat quarters are 18" x 21".

5 fat quarters of dark-blue batiks for blocks and outer border

5 fat quarters of periwinkle batiks for blocks and outer border

5 fat quarters of aqua batiks for blocks and outer border

3 yards of pale-blue batik for background, inner border, and binding

4 yards of fabric for backing

71" x 71" piece of batting

CUTTING

From *each* of the fat quarters, cut:
10 squares, 5" x 5" (150 total; 22 will be left over)

From the pale-blue batik, cut:
10 strips, 5" x 42"; crosscut into 80 squares, 5" x 5" (4 will be left over)

6 strips, 4½" x 42"

7 strips, 2½" x 42"

PIECING THE BLOCKS

1. Pair a dark-blue and a pale-blue 5" square, right sides together. Using a ¼" seam allowance, stitch on opposite edges of the squares. Cut the unit in half so that each piece measures 2½" x 5". Open each piece and press the seam allowances toward the dark-blue fabric.

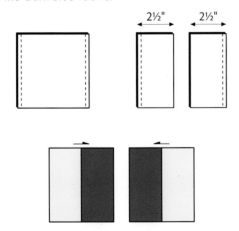

2. Place the two units right sides together, seams aligned, with *the light and dark fabrics opposite each other.* Stitch ¼" from the opposite edges. Cut the unit in half as shown.

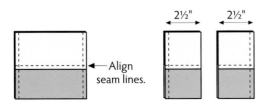

The inspiration for this quilt started with a beautiful fat-quarter pack that my sister-in-law purchased for me on Kaua'i. It reminded me so much of the waters of the island I love that I knew I had to create this quilt.

—Leanne

3. Press the seam allowances in one direction. Make a total of 24 four-patch units in this colorway. In the same manner, make 24 periwinkle and pale-blue units and 24 aqua and pale-blue units for a total of 72 four-patch units.

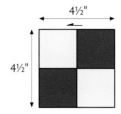

4. Referring to "Triangle Squares" on page 87, use dark-blue and pale-blue 5" squares to make a total of 24 triangle squares. In the same manner, make 24 periwinkle and pale-blue triangle squares and 24 aqua and pale-blue triangle squares for a total of 72 triangle squares.

5. Working with same-color units, sew two four-patch units and two triangle squares together as shown to make one block. Repeat to make 12 blocks in each colorway for a total of 36 blocks.

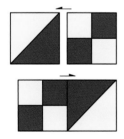
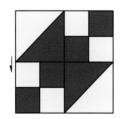

Make 36.

ASSEMBLING THE QUILT TOP

1. Arrange the blocks as shown in six rows of six blocks each.

2. Sew the blocks together in rows, pressing the seam allowances in opposite directions from row to row.

3. Join the rows. Press the seam allowances in one direction.

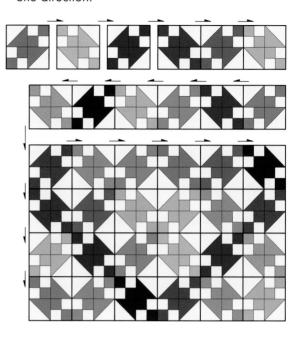

ADDING THE INNER BORDER

1. Sew the 4½" x 42" pale-blue strips together end to end and press the seam allowances open. From this long strip cut two strips, 48½" long, and sew them to the sides of the quilt top. Press the seam allowances toward the borders.

2. Cut two strips, 56½" long, and sew them to the top and bottom of the quilt top. Press the seam allowances toward the borders.

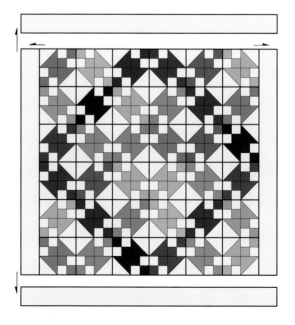

ADDING THE OUTER BORDER

1. Using four dark-blue 5" squares and four pale-blue 5" squares, make eight triangle squares.

Make 8.

2. With the remaining dark-blue, periwinkle, and aqua 5" squares, make 52 scrappy four-patch units.

3. Sew together six four-patch units, two triangle squares, and six more four-patch units to make one side border. Make two borders.

Side border.
Make 2.

4. Sew together seven four-patch units, two triangle squares, and seven more four-patch units to make the top and bottom borders.

Top/bottom border.
Make 2.

5. Sew the side borders to the quilt top. Press the seam allowances toward the inner borders. Sew the top and bottom borders to the quilt top. Press the seam allowances toward the inner borders.

FINISHING THE QUILT

1. Piece and trim the backing to measure approximately 6" larger than the quilt top.

2. Layer the backing, batting, and quilt top; baste. Quilt as desired. In keeping with the watery theme, this quilt has a wavy allover quilting design.

3. Trim the excess batting and backing even with the quilt top.

4. Use the 2½"-wide pale-blue strips to make and attach double-fold binding, referring to "Binding" on page 92. Label your quilt.

Piece a Backing to Match

You'll have a handful of leftover 5" squares and plenty of fabric from the fat quarters to cut more 5" squares—enough to incorporate into a pieced backing or a matching small lap quilt.

—Leanne

Blue Skies Ahead

Designed, pieced, and appliquéd by Adrienne Smitke; machine quilted by Dawna Callahan
Quilt size: 60½" x 68½" | **Block size:** 8" x 8"

MATERIALS

Yardage is based on 42"-wide fabric; fat quarters are 18" x 21".

14 fat quarters of assorted blue prints for blocks

7 fat quarters of assorted white-on-white fabrics for clouds

1 fat quarter of red fabric for birds

1⅛ yards of blue fabric for border and binding

4⅛ yards of fabric for backing*

1½ yards of 45"-wide fusible fleece for clouds

66" x 74" piece of batting

¼ yard of 20" fusible web for birds

Felt-tipped erasable fabric pen

8½" x 11" piece of clear template plastic

Curved quilter's safety pins (optional)

Consider a soft flannel for the backing to make this quilt extra cozy.

CUTTING

From *each* of the blue fat quarters, cut:
4 squares, 8½" x 8½" (56 total)

From the blue fabric for border and binding, cut:
7 strips, 2½" x 42"

7 strips, 2¼" x 42"

APPLIQUÉING THE BLOCKS

1. Using the appliqué patterns on page 49, trace and cut out one cloud and one bird from the template plastic. The cloud pattern has already been reversed for fusible appliqué.

2. On the fleece side of your fusible fleece, use the cloud template and your felt-tipped erasable fabric pen to trace 39 clouds. Cut out the clouds, leaving at least ½" beyond the drawn lines. Following the manufacturer's instructions, fuse six clouds each to the wrong side of six white-on-white fat quarters and three clouds to the wrong side of the seventh fat quarter. Cut out the clouds on the lines.

Guarantee blue patchwork skies year-round with a simple but sweet quilt featuring dreamy clouds and happy birds. Fusible fleece, adhered to the wrong side of the cloud fabric, keeps the blue background fabrics from showing through the white clouds. The fusible fleece also gives the appliqués structure so the clouds hold up to the machine quilting, and avoids the stiffness that fusible web can create. The appliqués are machine stitched, making the blocks quick and easy to put together.

—Adrienne

3. Use a curved quilter's safety pin to secure a cloud to the center of a blue square, positioning the cloud as shown. Using straight pins, pin the edges generously to secure. Referring to "Machine-Stitched Appliqué" on page 90 and using a blanket stitch or zigzag stitch, appliqué the cloud to the block. Repeat with the remaining white clouds for a total of 39 cloud blocks.

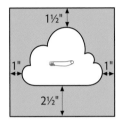 

Make 39.

4. Referring to "Fusible Appliqué" on page 89, use the bird template to trace one regular and one reversed bird onto the paper side of the fusible web. Cut out the birds, leaving at least ½" beyond the drawn lines. To keep the shapes supple, cut out the center of the birds, leaving a ¼" margin all the way around.

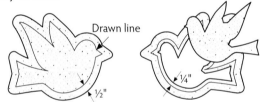

Drawn line

5. Following the manufacturer's instructions, fuse the birds to the wrong side of the red fat quarter. Cut out the shapes on the drawn lines and fuse each bird to a blue square. Appliqué each bird.

Make 1 and 1 reversed.

ASSEMBLING THE QUILT TOP

1. Lay out the blocks as shown or arrange them in any order you like. This is a great opportunity to personalize your quilt and make it your own!

2. Sew the blocks into horizontal rows. Press the seam allowances in opposite directions from row to row. Join the rows. Press the seam allowances in one direction.

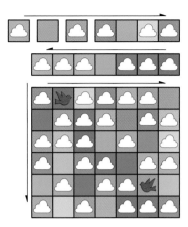

ADDING THE BORDER

1. Sew the seven blue 2½" x 42" strips end to end to make one long strip. Press the seam allowances open. Cut two strips, 64½" long, and sew to the sides of the quilt top. Press the seam allowances toward the borders.

2. Cut two strips, 60½" long, and sew to the top and bottom of the quilt top. Press the seam allowances toward the borders.

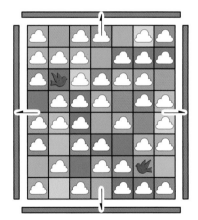

FINISHING THE QUILT

1. Piece and trim the backing to measure approximately 6" larger than the quilt top.

2. Layer the backing, batting, and quilt top; baste. Quilt as desired. Adrienne's quilt was machine quilted in an allover flower pattern. When the shapes were nested, they took on the appearance of fluffy, swirly clouds.

3. Trim the excess batting and backing even with the quilt top.

4. Use the 2¼"-wide blue strips to make and attach double-fold binding, referring to "Binding" on page 92. Consider using a leftover cloud as your label.

Bird
Cut 1 and 1 reversed from red.

Cloud
Cut 39 from white.
Pattern is reversed for fusible appliqué.

Berry Fine Wine

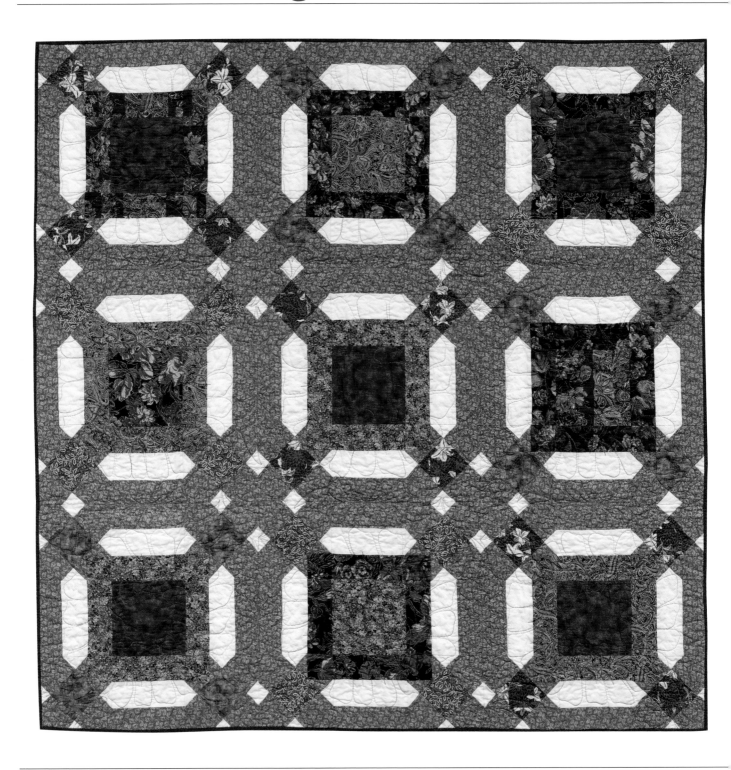

Designed and pieced by Cathy Valentine Reitan; machine quilted by Karen Burns of Compulsive Quilting

Quilt size: 54½" x 54½" | **Block size:** 18" x 18"

MATERIALS

Yardage is based on 42"-wide fabric; fat quarters are 18" x 21".

5 fat quarters of assorted berry- and wine-colored prints for blocks

3 fat quarters of turquoise prints for blocks

1 fat quarter of wine-colored solid for blocks

1¾ yards of brown print for blocks

1 yard of white fabric for blocks

⅝ yard of berry tone-on-tone for binding

3½ yards of fabric for backing

61" x 61" piece of batting

CUTTING

Plan your blocks before cutting by studying the quilt and pairing the fabrics into nine sets, one for each block.

From the solid wine-colored fat quarter, cut:
5 squares, 6½" x 6½"

From 4 of the berry- and wine-colored fat quarters, cut:
1 square, 6½" x 6½" (4 total)

From the berry- and wine-colored fat quarters, cut:
36 rectangles, 2½" x 6½", in 9 groups of 4 matching pieces
36 squares, 2½" x 2½", in 9 groups of 4 matching pieces

From *each* of the 3 turquoise fat quarters, cut:
12 squares, 2½" x 2½" (36 total)
12 squares, 3¼" x 3¼" (36 total); cut each square into quarters diagonally to yield 4 small triangles (144 total)

From the white fabric, cut:
36 rectangles, 2½" x 6½"
36 squares, 3¼" x 3¼"; cut each square into quarters diagonally to yield 4 small triangles (144 total)

From the brown print, cut:
36 rectangles, 2½" x 6½"
72 squares, 3¼" x 3¼"; cut each square into quarters diagonally to yield 4 small triangles (288 total)
108 squares, 2½" x 2½"

From the berry tone-on-tone fabric, cut:
7 strips, 2½" x 42"

The rich colors of a berry- and wine-colored pack of fat quarters, which included a border print, were just waiting to be combined and displayed. The setting is nontraditional: at first glance you might not realize that the quilt is made of rail-fence units and small star units. I added turquoise to the color combination for zing, and now I have an eye-catching throw or wall hanging.

—Cathy

PIECING THE RAIL-FENCE UNITS

Sew wine, white, and brown 2½" x 6½" rectangles together as shown to make a rail-fence unit. Press the seam allowances away from the white rectangle. Make four matching units for each block, for a total of 36 units.

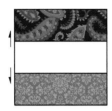

Make 36.

PIECING THE STAR UNITS

1. Sew a brown triangle to a white triangle as shown. Make 144 units. Sew a brown triangle to a turquoise triangle. Make 144 units. Press the seam allowances toward the brown triangles.

Make 144.   Make 144.

Practice First

Because the triangle units are directional, I found it helpful to make a practice unit for reference.

—Cathy

2. Sew the units from step 1 together as shown, matching the center seams. Make 144 units.

Make 144.

3. For each star unit, arrange matching triangle-square units and squares as shown into three rows, noting the position of the one wine-colored square and making sure the turquoise triangles are next to the turquoise square. Sew the units together in rows. Press the seam allowances toward the squares. Join the rows. Press the seam allowances in one direction. Make 36 star units.

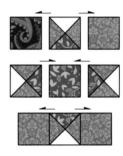 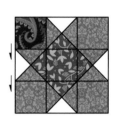

Make 36.

ASSEMBLING THE BLOCKS

1. *With the turquoise and wine-colored prints matching,* sort the units into nine groups with four of each unit and one 6½" square in each group.

2. Arrange four rail-fence units and four star units in three rows as shown, making sure the small wine-colored squares touch the matching rail-fence units. Sew the units together in rows. Press

the seam allowances toward the rail-fence units. Join the rows. Press the seam allowances in one direction. Make nine blocks.

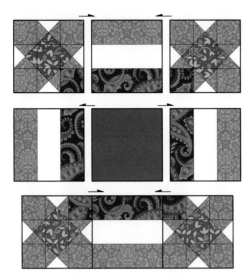

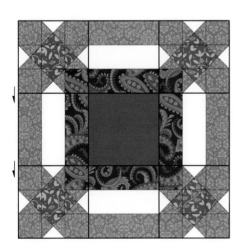

Make 9.

ASSEMBLING THE QUILT TOP

1. Arrange the blocks in three rows of three blocks each as shown, noting the placement of the solid and print center squares and alternating the turquoise prints from block to block.

2. Sew the blocks together in rows. Press the seam allowances in opposite directions from row to row. Join the rows. Press the seam allowances in one direction.

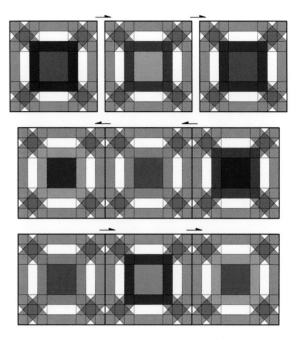

FINISHING THE QUILT

1. Piece and trim the backing to measure approximately 6" larger than the quilt top.

2. Layer the backing, batting, and quilt top; baste. Quilt as desired. In Cathy's quilt, free-form flower motifs fill each block.

3. Trim the excess batting and backing even with the quilt top.

4. Use the 2½"-wide berry tone-on-tone strips to prepare and attach double-fold binding, referring to "Binding" on page 92. Label your quilt.

Retrolicious!

Designed and pieced by Cornelia Gauger; machine quilted
by Cindy Glancy of Dancing Thread Long-Arm Quilting

Quilt size: 60½" x 80½" | **Block size:** 10" x 10"

MATERIALS

Yardage is based on 42"-wide fabric; fat quarters are 18" x 21".

2 fat quarters *each* of the following colors* (12 total): green, orange, red, blue, yellow, and pink for blocks

2 fat quarters of different black prints for blocks

2 fat quarters of different white prints for blocks

1⅛ yards of black-and-white print for blocks and borders

⅝ yard of black solid for binding

4⅞ yards of fabric for backing

67" x 87" piece of batting

*For each color, choose fat quarters that contrast in value—a light red and a medium red, for example.

CUTTING

See "Cutting Fat Quarters" on page 87.

From *each* of the 12 colored fat quarters, cut:

2 strips, 5½" x 18"; crosscut each strip into 3 squares, 5½" x 5½" (72 total)

2 strips, 3" x 18"; crosscut each strip into 6 squares, 3" x 3" (144 total)

2 strips, 1" x 12½" (24 total). From 2 of the fat quarters, cut 1 additional strip to make 26 *total* strips.

From *each* of the black and the white fat quarters, cut:

7 strips, 3" x 18"; crosscut into 42 squares, 3" x 3" (168 total; 1 square from each fat quarter will be left over)

From the black-and-white print, cut:

12 strips, 3" x 42"; cut 5 of the strips into:

    10 rectangles, 3" x 10½"

    10 rectangles, 3" x 5½"

    4 squares, 3" x 3"

From the black solid, cut:

8 strips, 2½" x 42"

I love how the black and white pathways run through this quilt, making the happy colors pop. The cutting and piecing are super easy; it's the color placement that's a bit tricky. Since each of the alternate blocks is different, instructions are given row by row, building the inner border in right along with the piecing.

—Cornelia

PIECING THE LARGE FOUR PATCH BLOCKS

Pair contrasting 5½" squares of each color—light green and medium green, for example—and sew together. Make two. Press the seam allowances toward the darker fabric. Join the units to make one large four-patch unit. Repeat to make three four-patch units in each color, for a total of 18.

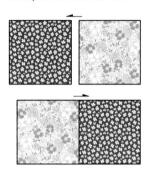 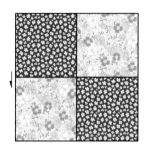

Make 3 in each color.

ASSEMBLING THE ALTERNATE BLOCKS

It's easier to place the colors correctly if you assemble the alternate blocks row by row. I also found it easier to join each row to the previous one as I went, but you may prefer to sew all the rows first, and then join them.

1. Pair 3" squares of each color and sew together. Make 12 in each color, for a total of 72 units.

Make 12 in each color.

2. Sew 3" white and black squares together as shown. Repeat to make a total of 17 units in those fabrics. Repeat with the remaining black and white squares for another 17 units. Sew two different units together to make 17 small four-patch units.

Make 17 of each.

Four-patch unit.
Make 17.

ASSEMBLING THE QUILT TOP

1. For row 1 (also the top inner border), join a black-and-white square, a black square, a green pair, a white square, a 10½" black-and-white rectangle, a black square, a yellow pair, a white square, a 10½" black-and-white rectangle, a black square, a red pair, a white square, and a black-and-white square.

Row 1

Location, Location!

Orient the black squares, white squares, and black-and-white four-patch units as shown throughout to create diagonal "chains" of alternating prints.

—Cornelia

2. For row 2, make two inner-border units as follows: For the left inner border, sew a black square and a white square to opposite ends of a green pair. For the right inner border, sew a white square and a black square to opposite ends of a red pair.

 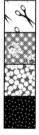

Make 1.   Make 1.

3. Make an alternate block for row 2, using two white squares, two black squares, a green pair, a pink pair, a yellow pair, a black-and-white

four-patch unit, and a 5½" black-and-white rectangle. Repeat, using one yellow pair, one green pair, and one red pair.

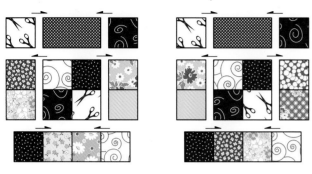

Make 1.   Make 1.

4. Assemble row 2 using the units made in steps 2 and 3, a large green four-patch unit, a large yellow four-patch unit, and a large red four-patch unit. Sew row 2 to row 1. Press the seam allowances toward row 1.

5. For row 3, make three alternate blocks as shown, paying careful attention to the placement of the pieces.

Make 1.   Make 1.

Make 1.

6. Assemble row 3 using a 10½" black-and-white rectangle at both ends, the alternate blocks from step 5, a large pink four-patch unit, and a large green four-patch unit. Sew this row to the first two rows. Press the seam allowances (and all subsequent horizontal seam allowances) toward the previous row.

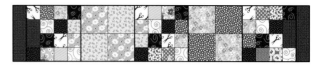

Row 3

7. Assemble and attach rows 4–8 in the same manner, making the alternate blocks as you go.

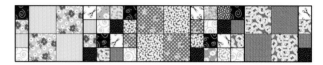

Row 4

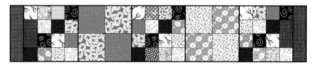

Row 5

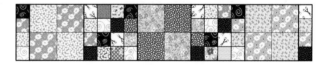

Row 6

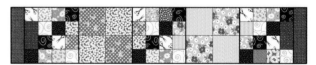

Row 7

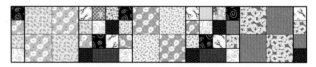

Row 8

8. For row 9 (the bottom inner border), assemble the pieces as shown and sew to row 8.

Row 9

ADDING THE BORDER

1. Sew three black-and-white 3" x 42" strips together and press the seam allowances open. Cut two strips, 55½" long, and sew to the top and bottom of the quilt top. Press the seam allowances toward the borders.

2. Sew the remaining four black-and-white 3" x 42" strips together and press the seam allowances open. Cut two strips, 80½" long, and sew to the sides of the quilt top. Press the seam allowances toward the borders.

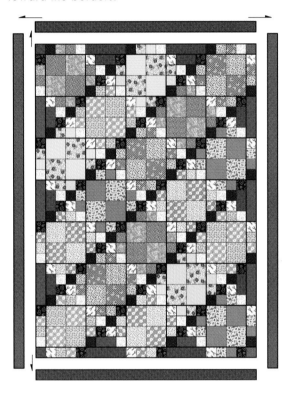

3. To create the faux piping just inside the binding, sew seven colored 1" x 12½" strips together, end to end. Press the seams allowances open, and then press the strip in half lengthwise, wrong sides together. Make two strips.

Make 2.

4. Using washable fabric glue or a long stitch, baste a piping strip to each side of the quilt top, aligning the raw edges of the piping with the edges of the quilt

top. Trim the piping strips even with the quilt top at both ends.

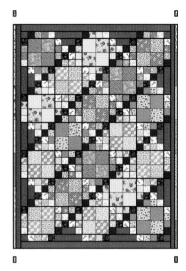

5. Repeat at the top and bottom of the quilt, using six 1" x 12½" strips for each.

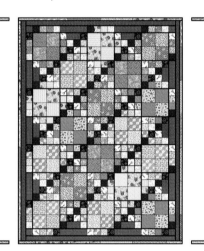

FINISHING THE QUILT

1. Piece and trim the backing to measure approximately 6" larger than the quilt top.

2. Layer the backing, batting, and quilt top; baste. Quilt as desired. Cornelia's quilt was machine quilted with an allover daisy pattern.

3. Trim the excess batting and backing even with the quilt top.

4. Use the 2½"-wide black strips to prepare and attach double-fold binding, referring to "Binding" on page 92. There should be just about ¼" of faux piping peeking out from underneath the binding, creating a "pop" of color to frame your quilt. Label your quilt.

Confectionery

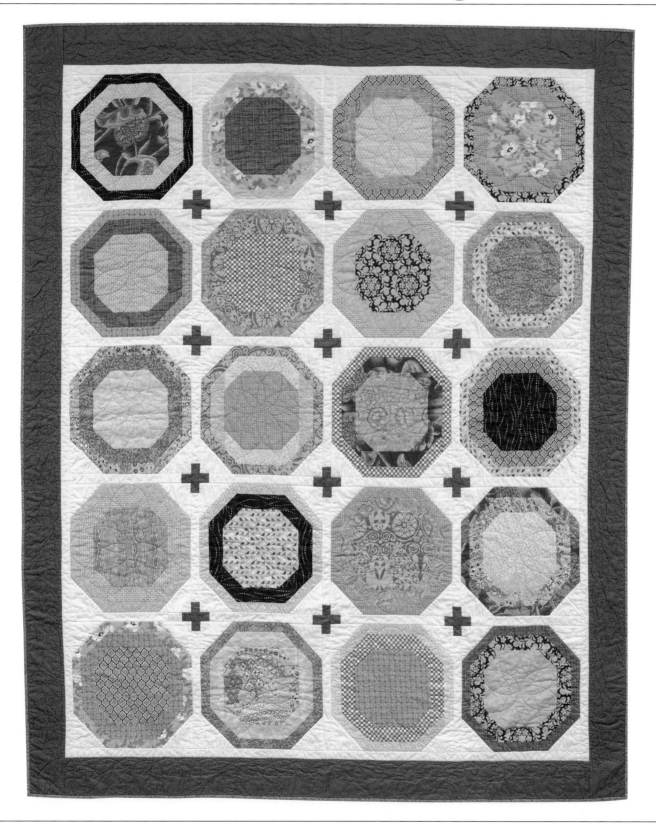

Designed by Adrienne Smitke; pieced by Judy Smitke and Adrienne Smitke;
machine quilted by Karen Burns of Compulsive Quilting

Quilt size: 65½" x 79½" | **Block size:** 13" x 13"

My original inspiration for this quilt came from those "everything-retro-is-cool-again" crocheted granny-square afghans. I wanted to replicate the rings of concentric color and the feeling of blocks stitched together on a neutral background. However, after selecting the brightest fat quarters from my stash, I realized the quilt didn't look like a retro-modern afghan at all. It reminded me of candy! Bright, colorful jawbreakers; gumballs; and, most of all, Everlasting Gobstoppers (those round candies that change colors as you suck on them). Pick your own scrappy palette of fat quarters inspired by something sweet (whether it's candy or your grandma) and follow the cutting diagram carefully, because this clever quilt doesn't waste an inch of fabric!

—Adrienne

MATERIALS

Yardage is based on 42"-wide fabric; fat quarters are 18" x 21".

20 fat quarters in a variety of colors for blocks

2 yards of white solid or print for sashing and inner border

1¼ yards of gray solid or print for sashing and outer border

⅝ yard of teal fabric for binding

4 yards of fabric for backing

71" x 85" piece of batting

CUTTING

From *each* of the fat quarters, use the cutting diagram on page 61 to cut*:
1 square, 8½" x 8½"

2 strips, 2" x 8½"

2 strips, 2" x 11½"

4 squares, 2½" x 2½"

2 strips, 1½" x 11½"

2 strips, 1½" x 13½"

4 squares, 3½" x 3½"

From the white fabric, cut:
80 squares, 4" x 4"

17 strips, 1½" x 11½"

14 strips, 1½" x 12½"

7 strips, 1½" x 42"

From the gray fabric, cut:
24 squares, 1½" x 1½"

12 rectangles, 1½" x 3½"

7 strips, 4½" x 42"

From the teal fabric, cut:
8 strips, 2¼" x 42"

*Refer to the first part of the cutting diagram below to cut each of the 20 fat quarters into the strips shown. Cut the strips into

pieces for the blocks as shown in the second part of the diagram. Organize the pieces into sets based on their dimensions.

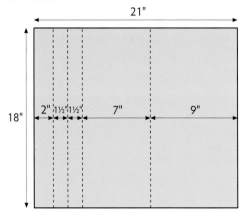

Cut into strips.

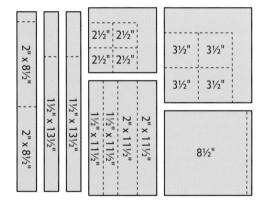

Cut strips into remaining pieces as shown.

MAKING THE BLOCKS

1. Referring to "Folded Corners" on page 88, mark the wrong side of four 2½" squares for the block inner ring. Sew the squares to a different-colored 8½" center square. Trim and press the seam allowances toward the corners.

2. Sew 2" x 8½" strips that match the corner squares in step 1 to both sides of the unit. Press the seam allowances away from the block center. Sew matching 2" x 11½" strips to the top and bottom of the unit. Press.

3. Using four 3½" squares in a different color, repeat step 1.

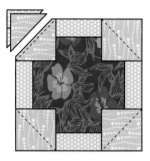

4. Sew matching 1½" x 11½" strips to the sides of the block. Press the seam allowances away from the block center. Sew matching 1½" x 13½" strips to the top and bottom of the block. Press.

5. With four white 4" squares, repeat step 1. Make 20 blocks.

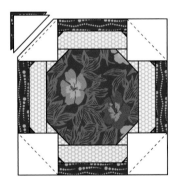

MAKING THE SASHING

1. Sew a gray 1½" square to the end of a white 12½" strip. Make six. Sew a gray 1½" square to each end of a white 11½" strip. Make nine. For both sets of sashing strips, press the seam allowances toward the gray squares.

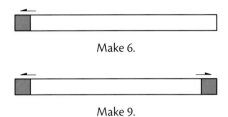

Make 6.

Make 9.

2. To make the sashing rows, sew two white 12½" strips, two white 11½" strips, and three gray 1½" x 3½" rectangles end to end as shown. Press the seam allowances toward the gray rectangles. Make four rows.

Make 4.

3. Find the center of each gray rectangle by folding it in half and marking the center with a pin.

ASSEMBLING THE QUILT

1. Sew four blocks and three matching sashing strips into rows to make two top/bottom rows with single gray squares in the sashing strips and three center rows with gray squares at both ends of the sashing strips. Press the seam allowances toward the blocks.

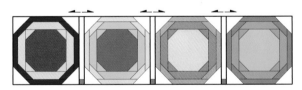

Top/bottom row.
Make 2.

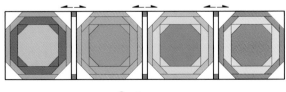

Center row.
Make 3.

2. Mark the centers of the gray squares in the sashing of the block rows with pins.

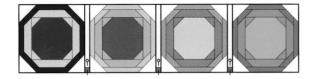

3. Arrange the block and sashing rows as shown.

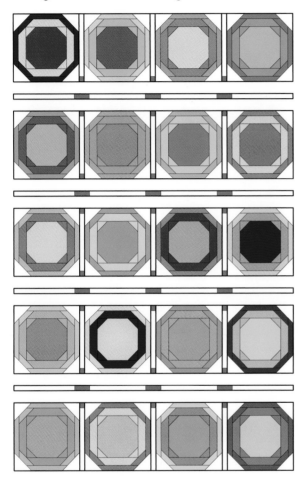

4. Sew the block and sashing rows together, matching the centers of the gray squares in the block rows with the centers of the gray rectangles in the sashing rows. Press the seam allowances in one direction.

ADDING THE BORDERS

1. Join the seven white 1½" x 42" strips end to end to make one long strip. Cut two inner-border strips, 69½" long, and sew to the sides of the quilt top. Press the seam allowances toward the inner borders. Cut two inner-border strips, 57½" long, and sew to the top and bottom. Press the seam allowances toward the inner borders.

2. Join the seven gray 4½" x 42" strips end to end to make one long strip. Cut two outer-border strips, 71½" long, and attach to the sides of the quilt top. Press the seam allowances toward the outer borders. Cut two outer-border strips, 65½" long, and attach to the top and bottom. Press the seam allowances toward the outer borders.

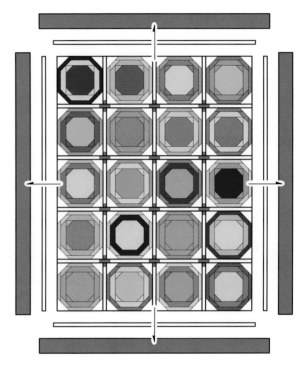

FINISHING THE QUILT

1. Piece and trim the backing to measure approximately 6" larger than the quilt top.

2. Layer the backing, batting, and quilt top; baste. Quilt as desired. Each of the blocks in Adrienne's quilt was machine quilted in a pattern of concentric circles. The gray borders were quilted in whimsical loops.

3. Trim the excess batting and backing even with the quilt top.

4. Use the 2¼"-wide teal strips to make and attach double-fold binding, referring to "Binding" on page 92. Label your quilt.

Grandmother's Thimble

Designed and pieced by Regina Girard; machine quilted by Karen Burns of Compulsive Quilting

Quilt size: 77" x 86" | **Block sizes: Snowball:** 4½" x 4½"

Nine Patch: 4½" x 4½" | **Small Thimble:** 3" tall | **Large Thimble:** 4¼" tall

MATERIALS

Yardage is based on 42"-wide fabric; fat quarters are 18" x 21".

10 assorted fat quarters for large and small Thimble blocks

5 light fat quarters for Snowball blocks

4 light fat quarters for Nine Patch blocks

4 dark fat quarters for Nine Patch blocks

3 dark fat quarters for Snowball blocks

2⅝ yards of dark-brown fabric for outer border and binding

5¼ yards of fabric for backing

83" x 92" piece of batting

8½" x 11" piece of template plastic

CUTTING

To avoid confusion, group the light and dark fat quarters used for each of the three different blocks before cutting.

Snowball Blocks

From *each* light fat quarter, cut:
3 strips, 5" x 21"; crosscut each strip into 4 squares, 5" x 5" (60 total)

From *each* dark fat quarter, cut:
8 strips, 2" x 21"; crosscut each strip into 10 squares, 2" x 2" (240 total)

Nine Patch Blocks

From *each* light fat quarter, cut:
7 strips, 2" x 21" (28 total)

From *each* dark fat quarter, cut:
8 strips, 2" x 21" (32 total)

Thimble Blocks

Use the template plastic to make large and small Thimble templates from the patterns on page 70. You'll need a total of 80 large Thimbles and 144 small Thimbles.

From *each* of the assorted fat quarters, cut:
1 strip, 4¾" x 21"; crosscut into 5 large Thimbles (50 total)

1 strip, 4¾" x 21"; crosscut into 3 large Thimbles (30 total)

2 strips, 3½" x 21"; crosscut into 12 small Thimbles (120 total)

From the remainder of *each* fat quarter, cut:
2 small Thimbles (20 total)

Continued on page 66

I have several antique thimbles that my grandmother used when stitching or darning. Although I don't hand stitch myself, I love having those reminders of my grandmother's handwork around. For this quilt, I combined my two favorite antique blocks, Snowball and Nine Patch, with a Tumbler/Thimble block. I used my collection of Japanese Daiwabo taupe fabrics, and I am thrilled with the result.

—Regina

From the leftover fabric scraps, cut:
4 total additional small Thimbles*

You may be able to cut only partial Thimbles if your fabric is less than 22" wide. Use these partial Thimbles on the ends of the strips for constructing the center; it will be trimmed square later.

Outer Border

From the *lengthwise grain* of the dark-brown fabric, cut:
2 strips, 7½" x 72"

2 strips, 7½" x 77"

4 strips, 2½" x 90"

PIECING THE NINE PATCH BLOCKS

Pair your fabrics for the Nine Patch blocks, one light and one dark, to make four sets of fabrics.

1. Sew a light 2" x 21" strip between two dark 2" x 21" strips to make strip set A. Press the seam allowances toward the dark strips. Repeat to make three of strip set A. Crosscut each strip set into 2" units, for a total of 30 units.

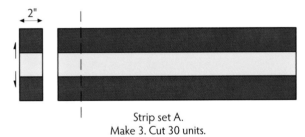

Strip set A.
Make 3. Cut 30 units.

2. Sew a dark 2" x 21" strip between two light 2" x 21" strips to make strip set B. Press the seam allowances toward the dark strips. Repeat to make two of strip set B. Crosscut each strip set into 2" units, for a total of 15 units.

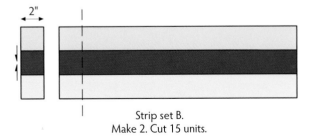

Strip set B.
Make 2. Cut 15 units.

3. Lay out two A units with one B unit as shown to form a Nine Patch block. Join the rows, being

careful to nest the seam intersections. Press the seam allowances toward the A units. Repeat to make 15 Nine Patch blocks for each set of fabrics, for a total of 60 Nine Patch blocks.

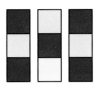

Make 60.

PIECING THE SNOWBALL BLOCKS

Refer to "Folded Corners" on page 88 to make the Snowball blocks using the 2" and 5" squares. For an alternative method, see the tip below. Make 60 total 5" Snowball blocks.

Make 60.

Fast Snowballs

If you don't want to take the time to mark the diagonal lines on the 2" squares, mark your sewing machine instead (shocking, I know). I used a permanent marker to draw a line straight out from my needle to the 0 mark on my sewing-machine table. If you don't want to mark on your machine, you can also use removable tape.

When sewing your 2" squares onto the 5" background square, start at the corner. Use the marked or taped line to keep your sewing line straight by keeping the lower point of the small square on the line.

—Regina

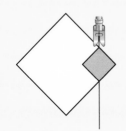

MAKING THE CENTER THIMBLE SECTION

It may look difficult to sew these Thimble blocks together, but it's easy once you get the hang of it.

1. Align two small Thimbles side by side, one with the narrow end at the top and one with the wide end at the top.

2. Flip the right Thimble over onto the left Thimble, keeping the right edges aligned. The measurement from the point of the bottom Thimble to the overlapping edge of the top Thimble should be ¼", as shown.

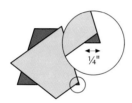

3. Sew using a ¼" seam allowance.

4. In the same manner, join a total of 12 Thimbles in a horizontal row, alternating their placement so they nest. Repeat to make 12 horizontal rows.

Make 12.

5. Arrange the rows, flipping every other row so the wide bottom of one Thimble touches the wide top of the Thimble in the next row. Press the seam allowances in opposite directions from row to row. Sew the rows together, being careful to butt the seam intersections. Press the seam allowances up.

6. Using a rotary cutter and long ruler, trim the section to 27½" wide.

27½"

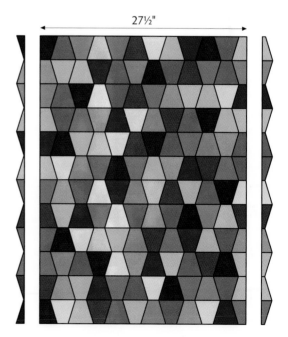

MAKING THE NINE PATCH AND SNOWBALL SECTIONS

1. Sew one Nine Patch block between two Snowball blocks. Press the seam allowances toward the Nine Patch block. Repeat to make a total of eight rows.

Make 8.

2. Sew one Snowball block between two Nine Patch blocks. Press the seam allowances toward the Nine Patch blocks. Repeat to make a total of eight rows.

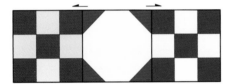

Make 8.

3. Alternate four of the Snowball rows with four of the Nine Patch rows. Sew the rows into a vertical section. Press the seam allowances down. Make another section and press the seam allowances up.

Make 2.

4. Attach the sections to the Thimble center as shown, with a Snowball row at the top of the left section and a Nine Patch row at the top of the right section. Press the seam allowances toward the Thimbles.

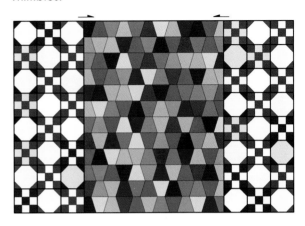

5. Arrange six Snowball blocks and six Nine Patch blocks into a horizontal row, alternating the blocks and placing a Nine Patch on the left end and a Snowball block on the right end. Sew the blocks together in a row. Press the seam allowances toward the Nine Patch blocks. Repeat to make a total of six rows.

Make 6.

6. Sew three rows together as shown to make the top section. Press the seam allowances down. Sew the remaining three rows together to make the bottom section.

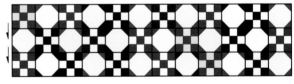

Make 2.

7. Attach the sections to the top and bottom edges of the quilt top, flipping the second section to align the Snowball/Nine Patch pattern running up and

down. Press the seam allowances toward the center section.

MAKING THE LARGE THIMBLE BORDER

1. Arrange 20 of the large Thimbles in a horizontal row. Sew the Thimbles together. Press the seam allowances in one direction. Repeat to make a total of four border rows.

Make 4.

2. Trim the ends of two borders to measure 63½". Sew a border to each side of the quilt top. Press the seam allowances toward the border.

3. Trim the ends of each remaining border to measure 63". Sew to the top and bottom of the quilt top. Press the seam allowances toward the border.

MAKING THE OUTER BORDER

Sew the 7½" x 72" border strips to the sides of the quilt top. Press the seam allowances toward the outer border. Sew the 7½" x 77" border strips to the top and bottom. Press the seam allowances toward the outer border.

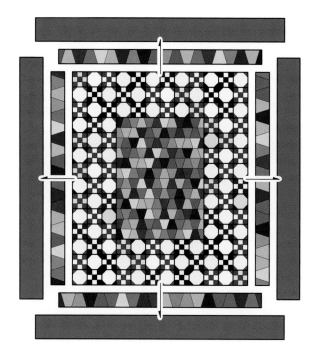

FINISHING THE QUILT

1. Piece and trim the backing to measure approximately 6" larger than the quilt top.

2. Layer the backing, batting, and quilt top; baste. Quilt as desired. Regina's quilt was machine quilted with a large feathered, leafy vine design that echoes motifs in the fabrics.

3. Trim the excess batting and backing even with the quilt top.

4. Use the 2½"-wide dark-brown strips to make and attach double-fold binding, referring to "Binding" on page 92. Label your quilt.

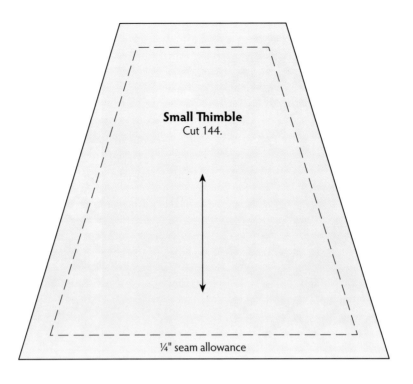

Small Thimble
Cut 144.

¼" seam allowance

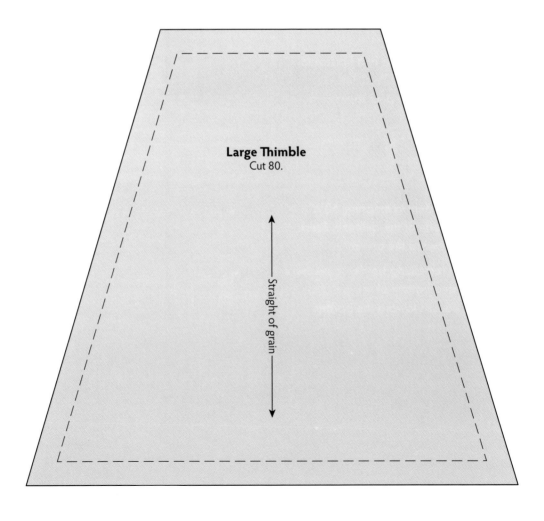

Large Thimble
Cut 80.

Straight of grain

Not Manly Enough

Designed and pieced by Robin Strobel; machine quilted by Karen Burns of Compulsive Quilting

Quilt size: 62½" x 72½" | **Block size:** 5" x 5"

I originally made this quilt for a friend's condo, but the colors weren't manly enough for him. That was OK! This quilt goes together so quickly that I simply made him another quilt in all neutrals and got to keep this one.

—Robin

MATERIALS

Yardage is based on 42"-wide fabric; fat quarters are 18" x 21".

18 fat quarters of assorted tan and brown prints for blocks

6 fat quarters of assorted turquoise prints for blocks

1¾ yards of dark-turquoise print for outer border and binding

⅜ yard of tan print for inner border

3¾ yards of fabric for backing (crosswise seam)

68" x 78" piece of batting

CUTTING

From *each* of the fat quarters, cut:
5 rectangles, 3½" x 5½" (120 total)

10 rectangles, 1½" x 5½" (240 total)*

From the tan print, cut:
6 strips, 1½" x 42"

From the dark-turquoise print, cut:
7 strips, 5½" x 42"

7 strips, 2½" x 42"

Keep rectangles of the same fabric together.

Fabric Choices

Choose three to five brown or tan fabrics for every turquoise one. I started with a very pretty fat-quarter pack of Asian prints, and supplemented with lots of fat quarters discovered in fat-quarter bins at local quilt shops. I used a wide range of values but kept all of the brown and tan fabrics warm toned. I like the look you get when you use a lot of different prints, so I used more than the minimum of 24 fat quarters. So I could pretend to be thrifty, I pieced the leftovers to make the backing for my quilt.

—Robin

PIECING THE BLOCKS

Randomly sew matching 1½" x 5½" rectangles to both long sides of a 3½" x 5½" contrasting rectangle. Press the seam allowances toward the darker fabric. Make 120 blocks.

Make 120.

ASSEMBLING THE QUILT TOP

1. Arrange and sew the blocks in 12 rows of 10 blocks per row, alternating the direction of each block as shown. Press the seam allowances in opposite directions from row to row. Sew the rows together. Press the seam allowances in one direction.

2. Piece the 1½" tan-print strips end to end to make one long strip. From this, cut two side borders, 60½" long, and sew them to the quilt sides. Press the seam allowances toward the borders. From the remainder of the long tan strip, cut top and bottom borders, 52½" long, and sew them to the top and bottom of the quilt. Press the seam allowances toward the borders.

3. Piece the 5½" dark-turquoise strips end to end to make one long strip. From this strip, cut four strips, 62½" long, for the outer borders. Sew to the quilt.

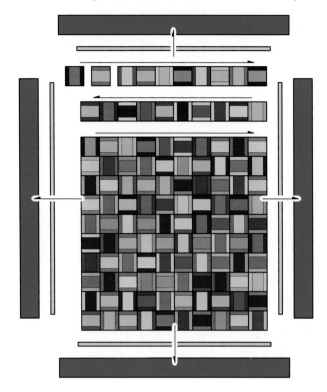

FINISHING THE QUILT

1. Piece and trim the backing to measure approximately 6" larger than the quilt top, or use leftover fabric to piece the back.

2. Layer the backing, batting, and quilt top; baste. Quilt as desired.

3. Trim the excess batting and backing even with the quilt top.

4. Use the 2½"-wide dark-turquoise strips to prepare and attach double-fold binding, referring to "Binding" on page 92. Label your quilt.

Remembering Chancellorsville

Designed and pieced by Abbi Barden; hand quilted by Cathy Reitan

Quilt size: 73" x 93" | **Block size:** 9" x 9"

MATERIALS

Yardage is based on 42"-wide fabric; fat quarters are 18" x 21".

12 assorted fat quarters for blocks

6 blue fat quarters for blocks and inner border

4 red fat quarters for blocks and vertical sashing

2¼ yards of dark print for outer border and binding

2 yards of cream print for setting triangles

5½ yards of fabric for backing

79" x 99" piece of batting

CUTTING

Sashing, Borders, and Binding

From the 4 red fat quarters, cut a *total* of:
12 assorted strips, 2½" x 21"

From the 6 blue fat quarters, cut a *total* of:
14 assorted strips, 2½" x 21"

From the cream print, cut:
10 squares, 14" x 14"; cut twice diagonally to yield 40 triangles

8 squares, 7¼" x 7¼"; cut once diagonally to yield 16 triangles

From the dark print, cut:
8 strips, 6½" x 42"

9 strips, 2½" x 42"

Inspired by Barbara Brackman's Civil War Reunion fabric collection by Moda, this quilt recognizes the organizations that work so diligently to preserve Civil War battlefield sites. The efforts of these dedicated groups save many of these historically significant places for the education and enjoyment of us all—and for future generations. Each of the six blocks in this project has been named for a battlefield, as has the quilt itself.

—Abbi

For Scrappy Blocks

Use different combinations of fat quarters for the blocks in each horizontal row. Try combining medium fabrics, medium-dark fabrics, and dark fabrics for value contrast, as well as mixing different colors.

—Abbi

Gettysburg Blocks

Cutting is for 1 block. You'll need 4 total.

From the first fat quarter, cut:
2 squares, 5⅜" x 5⅜"; cut in half diagonally to yield 4 triangles

From the second fat quarter, cut:
1 square, 4¼" x 4¼"; cut into quarters diagonally to yield 4 triangles

2 squares, 2⅜" x 2⅜"; cut in half diagonally to yield 4 triangles

Continued on page 76

From the third fat quarter, cut:
4 rectangles, 2" x 3½"

From the fourth fat quarter, cut:
1 square, 3½" x 3½"

Chickamauga Blocks

Cutting is for 1 block. You'll need 4 total.

From the first fat quarter, cut:
3 squares, 3⅞" x 3⅞"

3 squares, 3½" x 3½"

From the second fat quarter, cut:
3 squares, 3⅞" x 3⅞"

Vicksburg Blocks

Cutting is for 1 block. You'll need 4 total.

From the first fat quarter, cut:
5 squares, 3½" x 3½"

From the second fat quarter, cut:
4 squares, 3½" x 3½"

Manassas Blocks

Cutting is for 1 block. You'll need 4 total.

From the first fat quarter, cut:
1 square, 7¼" x 7¼ "; cut into quarters diagonally to yield 4 triangles

From the second fat quarter, cut:
4 rectangles, 2⅝" x 5⅝"

From the third fat quarter, cut:
1 square, 2⅝" x 2⅝"

Franklin Blocks

Cutting is for 1 block. You'll need 4 total.

From the first fat quarter, cut:
2 squares, 3⅞" x 3⅞"

4 squares, 3½" x 3½"

From the second fat quarter, cut:
2 squares, 3⅞" x 3⅞"

1 square, 3½" x 3½"

The Wilderness Blocks

Cutting is for 1 block. You'll need 4 total.

From the first fat quarter, cut:
4 squares, 3½" x 3½"

From the second fat quarter, cut:
2 squares, 4⅜" x 4⅜"

From the third fat quarter, cut:
2 squares, 4⅜" x 4⅜"

1 square, 3½" x 3½"

MAKING THE BLOCKS

Gettysburg Blocks

1. Sew 2" x 3½" rectangles to opposite sides of a 3½" square. Press the seam allowances toward the square. Add 4¼" triangles to the opposite sides of the rectangles. Press the seam allowances away from the rectangles.

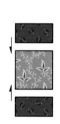  

Make 1.

2. Add a 2⅜" triangle to each short edge of a 2" x 3½" rectangle. Press the seam allowances toward the small triangles. Add a 4¼" triangle to the left edge of the unit. Press the seam allowances away from the rectangle. Make two.

Make 2.

3. Join the vertical rows. Press the seam allowances away from the center square.

4. Sew 5⅜" triangles to opposite sides of the unit. Press the seam allowances toward the triangles. Repeat with the remaining large triangles on the remaining sides of the unit. Make four blocks.

Make 4.

Chickamauga Blocks

1. Referring to "Triangle Squares" on page 87, make six triangle squares using the different 3⅞" squares. Press the seam allowances toward the darker fabric.

Make 6.

2. Lay out the triangle squares and the 3½" squares in three rows as shown. Sew the squares together in each row. Press the seam allowances in opposite directions from row to row. Join the rows. Press the seam allowances away from the center row. Make four blocks.

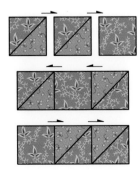 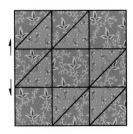

Make 4.

Vicksburg Blocks

Lay out the contrasting 3½" squares into three rows as shown. Sew the squares together in each row. Press the seam allowances in opposite directions from row to row. Join the rows. Press the seam allowances away from the center row. Make four blocks.

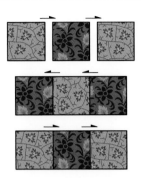 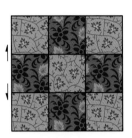

Make 4.

Manassas Blocks

1. Lay out the triangles, rectangles, and center square as shown. (The rectangles will extend beyond the corners; you'll trim them once the block is sewn.)

2. Sew the pieces together in diagonal rows. Press the seam allowances toward the rectangles in each row. Join the rows. Press the seam allowances away from the center row.

3. Using a rotary ruler and cutter, trim the rectangles to make the block square. Make four blocks.

Make 4.

Franklin Blocks

1. Referring to "Triangle Squares," make four triangle squares using the contrasting 3⅞" squares. Press the seam allowances toward the darker fabric.

2. Lay out the triangle squares and the 3½" squares in three rows as shown. Sew the squares together in each row. Press the seam allowances in opposite directions from row to row. Join the rows. Press the seam allowances away from the center row. Make four blocks.

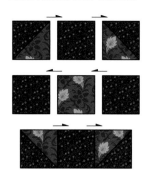 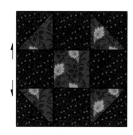

Make 4.

The Wilderness Blocks

1. Pin two contrasting 4⅜" squares right sides together. Draw a line diagonally from corner to corner on the lighter square. Stitch ¼" on either side of the line. Cut the unit on the *unmarked* corner-to-corner diagonal; then cut on the marked line to create four units. Press the seam allowances toward the darker fabric.

2. Pair two units as shown and stitch together on the diagonal edges. Press and square up the unit to 3½". Repeat with the remaining two 4⅜" squares for a total of four units.

Make 4.

3. Lay out the units made in step 2 and the 3½" squares in three rows as shown. Sew the pieces together in each row. Press the seam allowances in opposite directions from row to row. Join the rows. Press the seam allowances away from the center row. Make four blocks.

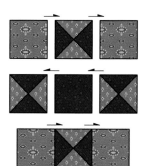 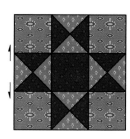

Make 4.

ASSEMBLING THE QUILT TOP

1. Arrange the blocks and the cream 14" setting triangles as shown. Sew the blocks and triangles together in diagonal rows. Press the seam allowances toward the setting triangles. Add the cream 7¼" corner triangles to the top and bottom of each row. Press. Make four rows.

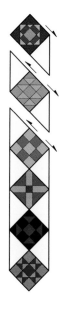 

Make 4.

2. Stitch the 12 red 2½" x 21" strips together end to end for the sashing. Measure each strip of assembled blocks from top to bottom through the center. Using the average of the four measurements, cut three sashing strips from the red strip. Join the block rows and the sashing strips, easing (see page 88) to fit as needed. Press the seam allowances toward the sashing strips.

3. Stitch the dark-print 6½" strips together end to end to make one long strip for the outer borders. Repeat step 2 to cut and attach the outer borders.

ADDING THE BORDERS

1. Stitch the blue 2½" x 21" strips together end to end to make one long strip for the inner borders.

2. Referring to "Adding Borders" on page 91, cut and attach the inner borders, noting that in the quilt shown, the top and bottom borders are added first, before attaching the side borders.
This means you'll measure the *width* of the quilt first to cut and add the top and bottom borders, and then measure the *length* to cut the side borders.

FINISHING THE QUILT

1. Piece and trim the backing to measure approximately 6" larger than the quilt top.

2. Layer the backing, batting, and quilt top; baste. Quilt as desired.

3. Trim the excess batting and backing even with the quilt top.

4. Use the 2½"-wide dark-print strips to prepare and attach double-fold binding, referring to "Binding" on page 92. Label your quilt.

Stars in the Garden

Designed and pieced by Stan Green; machine quilted by Krista Moser

Quilt size: 56½" x 56½" | **Block size:** 16" x 16"

MATERIALS

Yardage is based on 42"-wide fabric; fat quarters are 18" x 21".

2 fat quarters of yellow print for blocks

2 fat quarters of large-scale blue floral for blocks

2 fat quarters of large-scale pink floral for sashing and border

2 fat quarters of small-scale blue floral for blocks

2 fat quarters of small-scale green floral for border

1 fat quarter of black print for blocks

¾ yard of small-scale lime-green print for blocks and binding

½ yard of red print for border

½ yard of purple print for border

3½ yards of fabric for backing

63" x 63" piece of batting

CUTTING

From the black fat quarter, cut:
32 squares, 2½" x 2½"

From the small-scale lime-green print, cut:
32 squares, 2½" x 2½"
6 strips, 2½" x 42"

From the yellow fat quarters, cut a *total* of:
24 squares, 4⅞" x 4⅞"

From the large-scale blue-floral fat quarters, cut a *total* of:
24 squares, 4⅞" x 4⅞"

From the large-scale pink-floral fat quarters, cut a *total* of:
6 squares, 8½" x 8½"

From the small-scale blue-floral fat quarters, cut a *total* of:
5 squares, 8½" x 8½"

From the small-scale green-floral fat quarters, cut a *total* of:
6 squares, 8½" x 8½"

From the purple print, cut:
8 strips, 4½" x 16½"

From the red print, cut:
8 strips, 4½" x 16½"

A variety of values and colors establish the design in this garden-themed quilt. Although some of the prints are very large in scale, mixing them with small- and medium-scale patterns allows the large prints to stand out. Notice how the wide sashing almost becomes the primary pattern, with the stars playing a supporting role.

—Stan

PIECING THE STAR BLOCKS

1. Sew two lime-green and two black 2½" squares together as shown to make a small four-patch unit. Repeat to make a total of 16 four-patch units.

Make 16.

2. Referring to "Triangle Squares" on page 87, use the yellow and blue 4⅞" squares to make a total of 48 triangle squares.

Make 48.

3. Sew the triangle squares together in pairs with the blue edges adjoining as shown. Make 24 units.

Make 24.

4. Sew four of the four-patch units, four triangle-square units, and a blue 8½" square together as shown to complete a Star block. Press the seam allowances as shown. Join the rows. Press the seam allowances toward the center. Repeat to make four blocks.

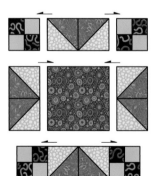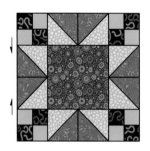

Make 4.

PIECING THE SASHING UNITS

Sew two blue/yellow units from step 3 of "Piecing the Star Blocks" and a pink 8½" square together to make a sashing unit. Press the seam allowances toward the pink square. Make four sashing units.

Make 4.

ASSEMBLING THE QUILT TOP

1. Lay out the Star blocks and sashing units as shown, with the remaining 8½" blue square in the center. Join the blocks and units into rows. Press the seam allowances as shown. Sew the rows together. Press the seam allowances toward the center row. Notice that the center blue 8½" square creates a fifth star in the middle of the quilt.

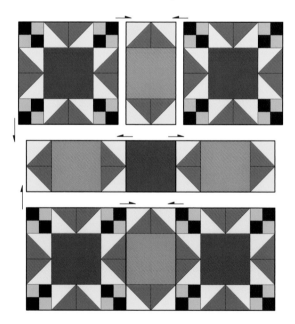

2. Sew the red and purple strips together to form eight pieced border sets.

Make 8.

3. Sew pieced border sets to the opposite edges of a green 8½" square. Press the seam allowances toward the borders. Make two units for the side borders.

Make 2.

4. Sew the borders to the sides of the quilt top. Press the seam allowances toward the borders.

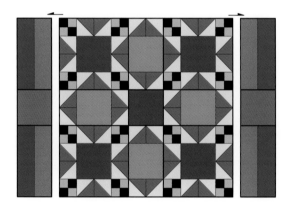

5. Sew two pieced border sets, joining two green 8½" squares, and a pink 8½" square as shown. Press the seam allowances toward the borders. Make two units for the top and bottom borders.

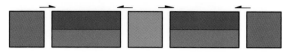

Make 2.

6. Sew the top and bottom borders to the quilt top. Press the seam allowances toward the borders.

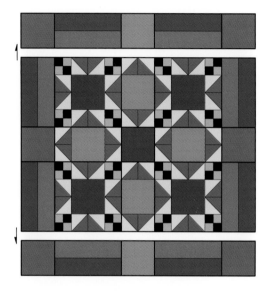

FINISHING THE QUILT

1. Piece and trim the backing to measure approximately 6" larger than the quilt top.

2. Layer the backing, batting, and quilt top; baste. Quilt as desired.

3. Trim the excess batting and backing even with the quilt top.

4. Use the lime-green 2½"-wide strips to make and attach double-fold binding, referring to "Binding" on page 92. Label your quilt.

Lost and Found

Pieced by Mary Green; machine quilted by Krista Moser
Quilt size: 48½" x 72½" | **Block size:** 12" x 12"

MATERIALS

Yardage is based on 42"-wide fabric; fat quarters are 18" x 21".

12 fat quarters of coordinating light and medium print for blocks

2⅝ yards of dark-purple print for blocks

⅝ yard of pink print for binding

3 yards of fabric for backing (crosswise seam)

54" x 78" piece of batting

CUTTING

From the dark-purple print, cut:
17 strips, 3½" x 42"; from 5 of the strips, cut a total of 48 squares, 3½" x 3½"

12 strips, 2" x 42"

From *each* fat quarter, cut:
3 strips, 3½" x 21"; from 1 of the strips, cut 4 squares, 3½" x 3½" (48 total)

2 strips, 2" x 21" (24 total)

From the pink print, cut:
7 strips, 2½" x 42"

PIECING THE BLOCKS

Make one pair of blocks (A and B) at a time using the dark-purple fabric and one of the fat-quarter fabrics.

1. Cut a dark-purple 3½" x 42" strip in half and sew the halves to 3½" strips of fat-quarter fabric. Press the seam allowances on one strip set toward the dark-purple fabric and the seam allowances on the other set toward the fat-quarter fabric.

2. Cut four 3½" units from each strip set, for a total of eight units. Keep the units separated into two piles based on the direction of the seam allowances.

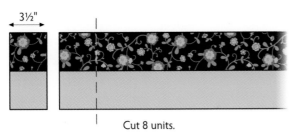

3½"

Cut 8 units.

The simple Carrie Nation block sparkles in this super-quick quilt. Thanks to the values reversing in alternate blocks, the diagonal chain seems to appear and disappear—to be lost and found. The blocks are made in pairs, and each fat quarter makes two blocks. For a less-scrappy look, purchase multiples of your favorite fat quarters. I used two of the green fabrics twice.

—Mary

3. Cut a 2" x 42" strip of dark-purple fabric in half and sew the halves to 2" strips of fat-quarter fabric. Press the seam allowances on both strip sets toward the dark purple. Cut eight 2" units from *each* strip set for a total of 16 units.

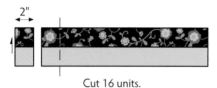

Cut 16 units.

4. Sew the 2" units together in pairs to make four-patch units. Make eight four-patch units.

Make 8.

5. To make block A, sew four dark-purple 3½" squares, the step 2 units with the seams pressed toward the dark-purple fabric, and four of the four-patch units together in rows as shown, making sure to orient the four-patch units correctly. Press the seam allowances toward the dark-purple fabric. Join the rows. Press the seam allowances in one direction.

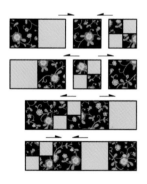 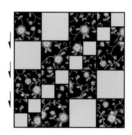

Block A

6. To make block B, sew four fat-quarter 3½" squares, the step 2 units with the seams pressed toward the fat-quarter fabric, and four of the four-patch units together in rows as shown above right. Again, make sure the four-patch units are oriented correctly. Press the seam allowances toward the fat-quarter fabric. Join the rows. Press the seam allowances in one direction.

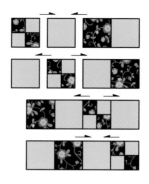 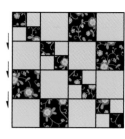

Block B

7. Repeat steps 1–6 to make a total of 24 blocks— one A and one B from each fat quarter.

ASSEMBLING THE QUILT TOP

Arrange the blocks in six horizontal rows of four blocks each. Sew the blocks together in rows. Press the seam allowances in opposite directions from row to row. You may need to re-press some of the block seams to get them to nest nicely. Join the rows. Press the seam allowances in one direction.

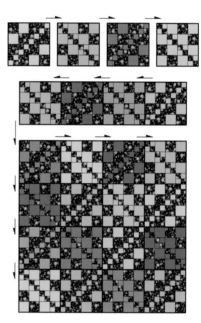

FINISHING THE QUILT

1. Piece and trim the backing to measure approximately 6" larger than the quilt top.

2. Layer the backing, batting, and quilt top; baste. Quilt as desired.

3. Trim the excess batting and backing even with the quilt top.

4. Use the 2½"-wide pink-print strips to make and attach double-fold binding, referring to "Binding" on page 92. Label your quilt.

Quiltmaking Basics

Whether you're new to quiltmaking or you're simply ready to learn a new technique, you'll find this quiltmaking-basics section filled with helpful information that can make putting your quilt together a pleasurable experience.

FAT-QUARTER FABRICS

All of the quilts in this book are based on fat quarters. The term *fat quarter* is used to describe a quarter yard of quilting cotton, but instead of being cut across the width of the fabric, a fat quarter is a half-yard cut of fabric that is cut in half along the fold to yield a piece that's approximately 18" x 21". A fat quarter offers the same square footage as a regular quarter yard (378" to be exact), but in a chunkier piece that's often more usable than a 9" x 42" skinny quarter.

Most quilt shops—brick-and-mortar and online—offer fat quarters. If you don't see the fabric you want in a precut fat quarter, it doesn't hurt to ask a shop employee. Many are willing to cut what you need, provided they carry fat quarters. They'll just add the other half of your half-yard cut to their lovely display of fat quarters for sale.

CUTTING FAT QUARTERS

Instructions for quick-and-easy rotary cutting are provided wherever possible. All measurements include standard ¼"-wide seam allowances. Just be aware that in a few of the projects, the cutting is specified for strips 18" long; others call for 21" strips. Be sure to cut in the correct direction when specified so that you can cut all the pieces you need without having to return to the quilt shop for another fat quarter!

MACHINE PIECING

Most blocks in this book are designed for quick piecing. Some blocks, however, require the use of templates for particular shapes, such as "Knockout Roses" on page 6. The template patterns for machine piecing include the required ¼"-wide seam allowances. Be sure to mark the pattern name and grain-line arrow on each template.

The most important thing about machine piecing is that you must maintain a consistent ¼"-wide seam allowance. Otherwise, the blocks won't be the desired finished size. If that happens, the size of everything else in the quilt is affected, including alternate blocks, sashings, and borders. Measurements for all components of each quilt are based on blocks that finish accurately to the desired size plus ¼" on each edge for seam allowances.

Chain Piecing

Chain piecing is an efficient system that saves time and thread. It's especially useful when you're making many identical units.

1. Sew the first pair of pieces from cut edge to cut edge using 12 to 15 stitches per inch. At the end of the seam, stop sewing but don't cut the thread.

2. Feed the next pair of pieces under the presser foot, as close as possible to the first. Continue feeding pieces through the machine without cutting the threads between the pairs.

3. When all the pieces are sewn, remove the chain from the machine and clip the threads between the pairs of pieces.

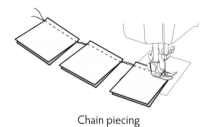

Chain piecing

Triangle Squares

A triangle square is made up of two half-square triangles sewn together. Here is a method for making triangle squares that are fast and accurate.

1. Cut the squares the size specified in the cutting list.

2. Draw a diagonal line from corner to corner on the wrong side of the lighter fabric. Layer two same-sized squares right sides together, with the marked

square on top and raw edges aligned. Sew ¼" on each side of the drawn diagonal line.

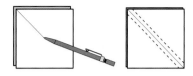

3. Cut on the drawn line. Press the seam allowances toward the darker fabric (unless instructed otherwise) and trim the dog-ears. Each pair of squares will yield two triangle squares.

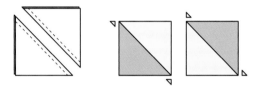

4. If your triangle squares need to be trimmed, use a square ruler to trim them to the correct unfinished size (3½" in the example below). Place the diagonal line of the ruler on the seam of the triangle square and trim two sides as shown. Rotate the block and trim the other two sides.

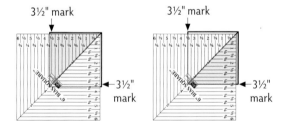

3½" mark

3½" mark

3½" mark

3½" mark

Folded Corners

Several of the projects in this book use the folded-corner technique.

1. Draw a diagonal line from corner to corner on the wrong side of a square. Position the square right sides together on one corner of a larger rectangle or square as shown so that the diagonal line goes from the top edge to the side edge. Stitch on the marked line.

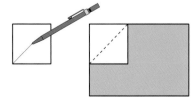

2. Press to set the stitches, and then trim the excess fabric in the corner, leaving a ¼"-wide seam allowance. Press the remaining triangle of fabric toward the corner.

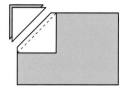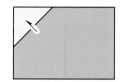

3. Continue as described in your project's instructions, using the folded-corner technique to add triangles to the corners of squares, rectangles, or strips.

Easing

If two pieces being sewn together are slightly different in size (less than ⅛"), pin the places where the two pieces should match, and in between if necessary, to distribute the excess fabric evenly. Sew the seam with the larger piece on the bottom. The feed dogs will ease the two pieces together.

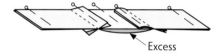

Excess

PRESSING

The traditional rule in quiltmaking is to press the seam allowances to one side, toward the darker color wherever possible. First press the seams flat from the wrong side of the fabric; then press the seam allowances in the desired direction from the right side. Press carefully to avoid distorting the shapes.

When joining two seamed units, plan ahead and press the seam allowances in opposite directions, as shown. This reduces bulk and makes it easier to match the seams. The seam allowances will butt, or "nest," against each other where two seams meet, making it easier to sew units with perfectly matched seam intersections.

Opposing seams

APPLIQUÉ BASICS

General instructions are provided for needle-turn, freezer-paper, and fusible appliqué. Even when a specific method of appliqué is mentioned in a project, you are always free to substitute your favorite method. Just be sure to adapt the pattern pieces and project instructions as necessary.

Making Appliqué Templates

To begin, you will need to make templates of the appliqué patterns. Templates made from clear plastic are durable, and because you can see through the plastic, it's easy to trace the templates accurately from the book page.

Place template plastic over each pattern piece and trace with a fine-line permanent marker. Don't add seam allowances. Cut out the templates on the drawn lines. You need only one template for each different motif or shape. Write the pattern name and grain-line arrow (if applicable) on the template.

Needle-Turn Hand Appliqué

In traditional hand appliqué, the seam allowances are turned under before the appliqué is stitched to the background fabric. Two traditional methods for turning under the edges are needle-turn appliqué and freezer-paper appliqué. You can use either method to turn under the raw edges, and then use the traditional appliqué stitch to attach the shapes to your background fabric.

1. Using a plastic template, trace the design onto the right side of the appliqué fabric. Use a No. 2 pencil to mark light fabrics and a white pencil to mark dark fabrics.

2. Cut out the fabric piece, adding a scant ¼"-wide seam allowance all around the marked shape.

3. Position the appliqué piece on the background fabric. Pin or baste in place. If the pieces are numbered, start with piece 1 and add the remaining pieces in numerical order.

4. Starting on a straight edge, use the tip of the needle to gently turn under the seam allowance, about ¼" at a time. Hold the turned seam allowance firmly between the thumb and first finger of one hand as you stitch the appliqué to the background fabric with your other hand. Use a

long needle—a Sharp or milliner's needle—to help you control the seam allowance and turn it under neatly. The traditional appliqué stitch is the blind stitch. Use it to sew your appliqué pieces to the background.

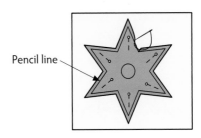

Pencil line

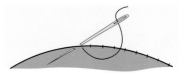

Appliqué stitch

Fusible Appliqué

Fusible web comes in different weights; a light-weight web works best for quilts. Always follow the manufacturer's instructions for fusing. Here are the basic steps in the process.

Reversed and Ready to Use

If the design is not symmetrical, the patterns in this book are reversed and are mirror images of the finished appliqué. This will result in your appliqué looking like the sample quilt.

1. Using the pattern provided, trace the shape onto template plastic and cut out on the drawn lines. Then trace around the plastic template onto the paper side of the fusible web. Cut out each piece approximately ¼" beyond the drawn line.

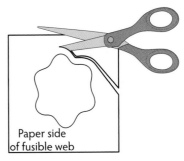

Paper side of fusible web

2. Position the fusible web, adhesive side down, on the wrong side of your appliqué fabric, leaving at least ¼" between each shape. Fuse as instructed by the manufacturer.

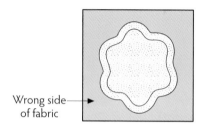

Wrong side of fabric

3. Cut out the prepared appliqué shapes on the marked lines.

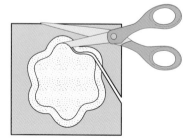

4. Remove the paper backing and position the appliqué on the background fabric. Fuse. If the pieces are numbered, start with piece 1 and add the pieces in numerical order. If one piece is overlapped by another, tuck it a scant ¼" under the edge of the top piece.

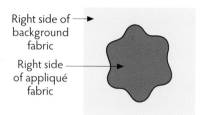

Right side of background fabric

Right side of appliqué fabric

Machine-Stitched Appliqué

You have several choices of thread and types of stitches that work well on fusible appliqué. One thread choice is monofilament. Unlike monofilament threads from the past, today's threads are soft and flexible, and they don't poke you with scratchy ends. Monofilament is almost invisible, and all it takes to secure the appliqué is a narrow zigzag stitch around each appliqué piece. Another choice is cotton thread in a color that matches the appliqué fabric.

Stitch with a narrow zigzag, buttonhole, blanket, or satin stitch around the appliqué pieces. Or, go for a little "zing" with a contrasting color of cotton or rayon thread paired with fancy decorative stitches, or a satin stitch.

Making Bias Stems

For several of the projects, you'll need to make stems using bias strips. Follow these basic instructions, starting with strips or narrow rectangles as specified in each project.

1. Fold each strip lengthwise, wrong sides together, to make a tube. Stitch using a ¼" seam allowance and trim the seam allowances to ⅛".

2. Center the seam on the back of the tube, allowing the seam allowances to lie flat in either direction, and press.

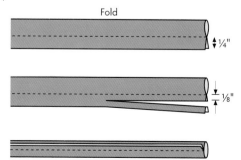

Fold

¼"

⅛"

SQUARING UP BLOCKS

When your blocks are complete, take the time to square them up. Use a large square ruler to measure your blocks and make sure they are the desired size plus an exact ¼" seam allowance on each side. For example, if you are making 9" blocks, they should all measure 9½" before you sew them together. Trim the larger blocks to match the size of the smallest one. Be sure to trim all four sides, or your block will be lopsided.

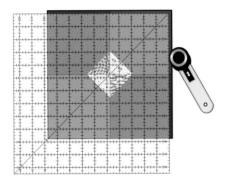

If your blocks aren't the required finished size, adjust all the other components of the quilt, such as sashing and borders, accordingly.

ADDING BORDERS

For best results, don't cut border strips and sew them directly to the quilt without measuring first. The edges of a quilt often measure slightly longer than the distance through the quilt center, due to stretching during construction. Instead, measure the quilt top through the center in both directions to determine how long to cut the border strips. This step ensures that the finished quilt will be as straight and as square as possible, without wavy edges.

Many of the quilts in this book call for plain border strips. These strips generally are cut along the crosswise grain and seamed where extra length is needed. However, some projects call for the borders to be cut on the lengthwise grain so that they don't need to be pieced.

1. Measure the length of the quilt top through the center. From the crosswise grain, cut border strips to that measurement, piecing as necessary. Determine the midpoints of the border and quilt top by folding in half and creasing or pinning the centers. Then pin the border strips to opposite sides of the quilt top, matching the center marks and ends and easing as necessary. Sew the border strips. Press the seam allowances toward the border strips.

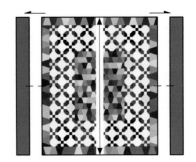

Measure center of quilt, top to bottom.
Mark centers.

2. Measure the width of the quilt top through the center, including the side border strips just added. From the crosswise grain, cut border strips to that measurement, piecing as necessary. Mark the centers of the quilt edges and the border strips. Pin the border strips to the top and bottom edges of the quilt top, matching the center marks and ends and easing as necessary. Sew the border strips. Press the seam allowances toward the border strips.

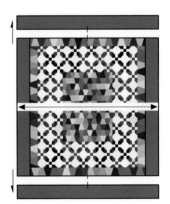

Measure center of quilt, side to side,
including border strips.
Mark centers.

QUILTING

Some of the projects in this book were hand quilted, others were machine quilted, and some were quilted on long-arm quilting machines. The choice is yours! For more information on hand or machine quilting, refer to ShopMartingale.com/HowtoQuilt.

FINISHING TECHNIQUES

Bind your quilt, add a hanging sleeve if one is needed, label your quilt, and you're finished!

Binding

All of the quilts in this book use a French double-fold binding. Cut strips across the width of the fabric. Binding strips cut 2½" wide will result in a finished binding that's slightly more than ¼" wide. (Some quilters prefer narrower binding, especially with a low-loft batting; see "Old Architectural Stars" on page 12.) You will need enough strips to go around the perimeter of the quilt, plus 10" for seams and to turn the corners.

1. Sew the binding strips together to make one long strip. Join strips at right angles, right sides together, and stitch across the corner as shown. Trim the excess fabric and press the seam allowances open to make one long piece of binding.

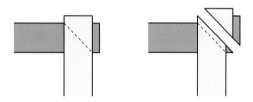

2. Fold the strip in half lengthwise, wrong sides together, and press.

3. If you plan to add a hanging sleeve, do so now before attaching the binding; see "Adding a Hanging Sleeve" on page 93.

4. Starting on one side of the quilt and using a ¼"-wide seam allowance, stitch the binding to the quilt, keeping the raw edges even with the quilt-top edge and leaving a 6" tail unstitched at the start. End the stitching ¼" from the corner of the quilt and backstitch. Clip the threads.

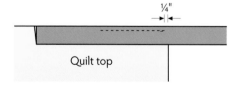

¼"

Quilt top

5. Turn the quilt so that you will be stitching down the next side. Fold the binding straight up, away from the quilt, making a 45° angle. Fold the binding back down onto itself, even with the edge of the quilt top. Begin stitching ¼" from the corner, backstitching to secure the stitches. Stitch to the next corner, stopping ¼" from the edge, and repeat the folding and stitching process. Repeat on the remaining edges and corners of the quilt.

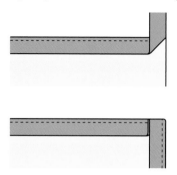

6. On the last side of the quilt, stop stitching approximately 7" from where you began. Remove the quilt from the machine. Overlap the ending binding tail with the starting tail. Trim the binding ends with a perpendicular cut so that the overlap is exactly the same distance as the cut width of your binding strips. (If your binding strips are 2½" wide, the overlap should be 2½"; for 2"-wide binding, the overlap should be 2".)

2½" overlap

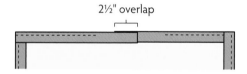

7. Open up the two ends of the folded binding. Place the tails right sides together so that they join to form a right angle, as shown. Mark a diagonal stitching line from corner to corner and pin the binding tails together.

Draw diagonal line.
Pin ends together.

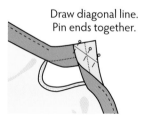

8. Stitch the binding tails together on the marked line. Trim the seam allowance to ¼"; finger-press the seam open to reduce the bulk. Refold the binding, align the edges with the raw edges of the quilt top, and finish sewing it in place.

9. Fold the binding over the raw edges to the back of the quilt, with the folded edge covering the row of machine stitching. Hand stitch in place, mitering the corners.

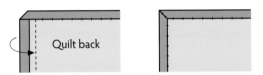

Adding a Hanging Sleeve

If you plan to display your finished quilt on the wall, be sure to add a hanging sleeve.

1. Using leftover fabric from the quilt backing, cut a strip 6" to 8" wide and 1" shorter than the width of your quilt. Fold the ends under ½", and then ½" again to make a hem. Stitch in place.

Fold ends under ½" twice.

2. Fold the fabric strip in half lengthwise, wrong sides together, and baste the raw edges to the top of the quilt back. The top edge of the sleeve will be secured when the binding is sewn on the quilt.

Baste sleeve to top edge of quilt.

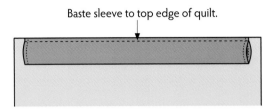

3. Finish the sleeve after the binding has been attached by blindstitching the bottom of the sleeve in place. Push the bottom edge of the sleeve up just a bit to provide a little give; this will keep the hanging rod from putting strain on the quilt.

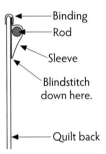

Signing Your Quilt

Be sure to sign and date your quilt. Future generations will be interested to know more than just who made it and when. Labels can be as elaborate or as simple as you desire. The information can be hand-written, typed, or embroidered. Be sure to include the name of the quilt, your name, your city and state, the date, the name of the recipient if the quilt is a gift, and any other interesting or important information about the quilt.

About the Contributors

Abbi Barden

Abbi began quilting in 1995, being first drawn in by the geometric aspect of the designs and all the beautiful fabrics available, and then by the wonderful community of quilters around the world who put aside their differences and join together in their enthusiasm for quilting. Abbi is a Customer Service Representative for Martingale; she's also active in a local guild and in a quilt-design group. She finds being surrounded by so much talent, generosity, and friendship very sustaining. She's interested in a wide range of quilt styles, both historical and contemporary. Such a wide variety of interests creates opportunities to collect a lot of fabric!

Mary J. Burns

Mary has always been interested in crafts of all kinds, and has been quilting since high school. With a background in advertising and marketing, she feels fortunate to work as Martingale's Marketing Coordinator and be surrounded by such inspiring creativity every day. She loves the camaraderie of quilting with friends at retreats, yet also enjoys the creative solitude of her sewing room at home. Amazingly, she hasn't yet been labeled a fabric hoarder by her quilt-enabling husband.

In addition to having fun with her college-aged sons and her cairn terrier, Rufus, Mary enjoys gardening, antiques, sports, movies, and the great outdoors. She and her husband live in their restored 1901 farmhouse in Snohomish, Washington.

Leanne Clare

Leanne has been working at Martingale for more than 11 years. An Account Manager, she enjoys working with shop owners around the country. She made her first quilt in 1968 as a high-school student—from the wrong kind of fabrics, with the wrong kind of batting, and using the wrong seam allowance. Plus she cut every piece individually with pinking shears (ouch!), and then tied the quilt with yarn. Leanne still has and treasures that first quilt.

She made her second quilt 12 years later for her first child. (That flannel baby quilt was very well used and has since completely fallen apart.) *Then* she took a class! Leanne has lost count of how many quilts she's made since, but the number is well into the hundreds. Most recently she made wedding quilts for both of her children and is now happily anticipating the first grandbaby quilt. Besides quilting, her other main passion in life is Hawaii, and if she's on vacation she's probably camping on a beach somewhere on the Islands.

Cornelia Gauger

Sewing and art did not come naturally to Cornelia. Her seventh-grade art teacher squelched any artistic tendencies, and her mother had to finish her eighth-grade sewing project so she wouldn't fail her home-economics class. This changed later when she happened into a quilt shop and was overwhelmed and delighted by all of the color and texture she found there. She was bitten by the quilting bug! Since then she's managed to complete several quilts, mostly as gifts for others. A self-proclaimed "Pointless Piecing Princess," she finds her quilting joy in simple construction, lots of color, being with friends while she sews—and no difficult points to match!

Cornelia has worked at Martingale for over 10 years, both as a Customer Service Representative and as an Account Manager.

Regina Girard

Regina was always the shy kid who was interested in art and crafts. She would draw and color Zentangles—complex, tangled patterns. She would also draw pictures from her coloring books—but sometimes upside down.

Regina got the urge to learn to quilt about 12 years ago, so she bought a sewing machine at a garage sale. The first pattern she made was a Mariner's Compass and she's still surprised that it came out round! She's made over 100 quilts since then, many of which she's given away to family, friends, and charity. Regina works as a Production Manager as well as a Book Designer for Martingale.

Mary V. Green

Since childhood, Mary has felt a strong urge to "make something," which over the years has led to many different creative pursuits. In her role as Editor in Chief, she now spends her days happily making books, a job that allows her to indulge in some of her favorite pastimes: reading, writing, and handcrafts.

Mary learned to sew as a child and taught herself to knit and crochet as a teenager, but she didn't discover quiltmaking until much later. Although she appreciates contemporary quilts, she loves traditional designs. The humble Nine Patch—the first block she ever made—is still her favorite, its many variations providing endless design possibilities.

Stan Green

Art has always been a force in Stan's life. As a child he spent hours sitting on the floor with his brother, sketching wildlife and landscapes from magazine photos. That early interest continued through college, where he studied fine arts and design. Over time, rug hooking, pottery, and photography replaced the fine arts. When his wife, Mary, started making quilts in the early 1990s, Stan thought that he would try his hand at designing blocks for her. He soon found that making the quilts himself was more exciting, and a new passion was ignited.

Stan was the Design Director at Martingale for 12 years before he retired to pursue his creative interests full time. He's strongly influenced by contemporary design, whether in quilting, rug hooking, or pottery, but has a deep appreciation for traditional designs as well.

Virginia Lauth

Virginia has been an avid quilter for many years. She loves to design and make quilts for her children and grandchildren, and enjoys hand quilting them as well. Virginia resides in Shoreline, Washington, with her husband, Marty. She works in the accounting department, and has been at Martingale for 19 years!

Nancy Mahoney

Author, teacher, editor, and fabric designer, Nancy has enjoyed making quilts for more than 20 years. She has authored 11 books and an impressive range of her beautiful quilts have been featured in over 90 national and international quilt magazines. When she's not designing and making quilts, Nancy enjoys traveling to guilds and events around the country, sharing her quilts, teaching her piecing and machine-appliqué techniques, and visiting gardens. She works as a freelance technical editor for Martingale.

Tracy Overturf

Tracy is the Key Accounts Representative in the customer service department at Martingale. Tracy and her best friend in elementary school, Laura, used to sew and wear matching outfits to school until they were teased so much they finally stopped. She was given her own sewing machine by her mother-in-law more than 32 years ago and is still sewing on it—even though it's now long past its 25-year warranty! Tracy began quilting when her daughter, Taylor, was born in 1988 and has developed some amazing friendships, all because of the love of quilting. Tracy credits her friends for pushing her to try new techniques and for oohing and aahing over the results no matter what! Quilting has truly enriched her life.

Cathy Valentine Reitan

Cathy has worked for Martingale for over five years. She started out in the marketing and sales department and moved into the position of Editorial Author Liaison in January 2008.

She's been sewing since she was 11 years old, progressing from fashion sewing to quilting. Cathy enjoys the entire quiltmaking process, from design to piecing to binding.

Adrienne Smitke

Adrienne grew up in a house full of handmade quilts and clothes. Her mother taught her to sew at an early age, even once assigning her sewing "homework" over summer vacation. She made a rad pair of black and neon green shorts (it was the '80s, after all). Drawing on her creative childhood, Adrienne studied illustration and graphic design in college, during which she finally began experimenting with sewing again on her own. Adrienne is Design Manager at Martingale. She coauthored her first book, *Everyday Handmade* (Martingale, 2011), with her friend Cassie Barden. You can see more of her patterns in *A Baker's Dozen* (2010), *Jelly Babies* (2011), and *Sew the Perfect Gift* (2011), also from Martingale.

Karen Costello Soltys

As the Managing Editor at Martingale, Karen has the opportunity to see firsthand all of the lovely quilts, knitted garments and accessories, and other items that arrive each week for publication. While it's all inspiring, she loves doing handwork and mainly spends her crafting hours knitting or hooking rugs. But when the quilting bug bites, she's most inspired by antique quilts and loves working with reproduction fabrics.

Karen is the author of *Bits and Pieces: 18 Small Quilts from Scraps and Fat Quarters* (Martingale, 2007).

Robin Strobel

As a new teacher in a very difficult school district, Robin began quilting as a form of self-therapy. "With high school students, you're never finished. There's always something more you can or should do, and I had a desperate need to do something creative that had a definite beginning and end. When you make a quilt, you not only get to play with fabric and color, you get a finished product! I needed that." She took many classes, learned many techniques, and eventually taught quilting at her local quilt shop. Robin doesn't quilt as endlessly as she used to, probably because she loves her job as an Illustrator and Editor at Martingale. She also knits, makes flame-worked glass beads, and is the servant for her two Scottish Fold cats.